Date Due			

Lee

ROBERT E. LEE

Born, Stratford Hall, Virginia, January 19, 1807
Graduated, Military Academy, Number 2, Class 1829
Married, Mary Custis, Arlington House, Virginia, June 30, 1831
Served in United States Army, 1825-1861
Won fame in Mexican War, 1846-1848
Offered command of United States Army, April 18, 1861
Resigned commission after Virginia seceded, April 20, 1861
Served in Confederate Army, 1861-1865
Given command Army of Northern Virginia, June 1, 1862
Noon of Career marked by Battle of Chancellorsville, May 1-4, 1863
The turning point was the Battle of Gettysburg, July 1-3, 1863
Surrendered to Grant at Appomattox, April 9, 1865
Installed as President, Washington College, October 2, 1865
Died at Lexington, Virginia, October 12, 1870

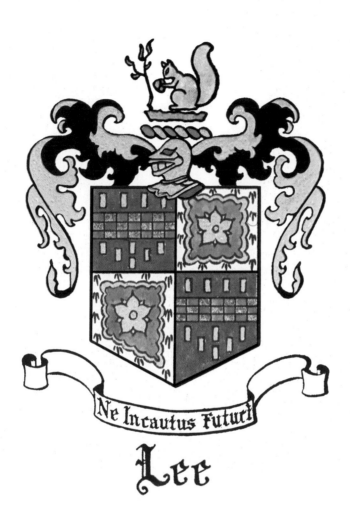

Ne Incautus Futuri

Lee

Robert Edward Lee—*in the dress uniform of a lieutenant of engineers from a portrait by William E. West at Baltimore, Maryland, March 1838. Courtesy, Lee Memorial Chapel, Washington and Lee University, Lexington, Va.*

The Story of Robert E. Lee

As told in his own words and those of his contemporaries

Edited by Ralston B. Lattimore

Source Book Series, No. 1, 1964

ILLUSTRATIONS

Note: *a single asterisk preceding an illustration title identifies the artist as Alfred R. Waud; a double asterisk indicates Edwin Forbes. All are from wartime originals in the Collection of the Library of Congress. All photographs of the Lee children are reproduced through the courtesy of Robert E. Lee's granddaughters, Mrs. Hunter de Butts, Upperville, Virginia, and Mrs. Hanson Ely, Richmond, Virginia.*

Cover: Gen. Robert E. Lee *as he appears in the Hoffbauer mural in the Battle Abbey, Richmond, Va. Reproduced through the courtesy of the Virginia Historical Society.*

Sketches for chapter headings by Jack Woodson, Richmond, Virginia.

Published by COLORTONE PRESS, Washington, D.C. 20009

in cooperation with the
Eastern National Park & Monument Association
© *Eastern National Park & Monument Association, 1964*

FIRST EDITION 1964
Library of Congress catalog card number 64-19183

This book was produced by Colortone Press, Washington, D. C. 20009.

The colorplates were made from color transparencies, the text was set in Intertype-Fotosetter
Times Roman, and the printing was done by lithography.
The text paper is Colophon 70 lbs. manufactured by the Curtis Paper Co.

CONTENTS

Maj. Gen. Henry ("Light Horse Harry") Lee—*father of Robert E. Lee, from a painting by Gilbert Stuart. Courtesy, Carter Lee Refo, Richmond, Virginia, owner.*

INTRODUCTION

Over the great span of history wars have many times threatened the existence of nations and even groups of nations. At these awful moments, almost invariably, singular men—sometimes good, sometimes evil—have come forward to lead their people to victory or to defeat.

One hundred years ago there was such a moment in the history of the United States. Divided by dissimilar economies, disturbed by the moral aspects of human slavery, inflamed by politicians, the people took sides against one another and the union of states fell apart. When eleven Southern states withdrew to form a new nation, the American Republic plunged into bitter civil war.

Now, in retrospect, after an intervening century, from the years of conflict and from the long painful period of readjustment which followed, the names of three men stand out above all others, Abraham Lincoln, Ulysses S. Grant, and Robert E. Lee. Had none of these men lived between 1860 and 1865, the destiny of the United States of America might have followed a far different evolutionary course. These three men were great Americans and their lives and deeds have had a profound effect on all Americans who have followed them.

In this small book we shall not pretend to relate the complete story of Robert E. Lee. His biography has already been written exceedingly well by others. We shall try, however, to present certain aspects of his life through the use of his own words and those of his contemporaries, which may help to reveal the special qualities he possessed, which in turn, set him apart from other men of his time.

No one today will deny Lee's claim to greatness, but he, himself, would have been the last man to have made such a claim. He led a rebel army in a civil war, yet he won a legendary place in the hearts of all of his countrymen. In the years to come, his fame will surely increase.

As a military genius Lee ranks near the top. Were it possible to choose a general staff from all military leaders of world history, he would undoubtedly be among the few selected. In his use of military intelligence to plan overall strategy, he was superlative. His only real deficiency as a soldier lay in the fact that notwithstanding his personal courage, he could never be ruthless, a qualification necessary for perfection in the martial profession. On an all-time general staff, Lee may not have been tapped for the position of chief, but he would have fit admirably in the "G-2" (Military Intelligence) position.

It is also quite probable that Lee might have excelled in other fields of endeavor had he not become a soldier. In the construction of vast fortifications at Atlantic seaports and in pioneer flood control work on the Mississippi River, he demonstrated unusual abilities in engineering. As superintendent of the Military Academy and as president of Washington College he combined administrative ability with marked success in the philosophy of teaching.

As a practicing Christian and spiritual leader of men, Lee was incomparable. Above all else, however, the secret of his greatness lies, perhaps, in the simple fact, that from the beginning to the end, he was a gentleman.

Ralston B. Lattimore

Ralston B. Lattimore

Fort Pulaski National Monument
Cockspur Island, Georgia

I. Young Man of Virginia

Lee spent most of his boyhood at Alexandria, Virginia, with occasional visits to Stratford, Chatham, Shirley, and other country estates of his Lee and Carter kin. He grew up in a town and countryside where George Washington was still a living memory and many of the Revolutionary heroes were related to him through ties of blood or marriage. He began his education at his mother's knee and when he was old enough he was sent to the family school for Carter boys maintained at Eastern View in Fauquier County, the home of his aunt, Mrs. Robert Randolph. About 1820, he entered the Alexandria academy for three years of study in mathematics, Greek and Latin.

Seventy-five years after the birth of Washington, Robert Edward, the fourth son of General Henry Lee and Anne Hill Carter, was born at Stratford, Westmoreland County, Virginia, on the 19th of January 1807. If he inherited much from a long and illustrious line of paternal ancestors, he no less fell heir to the strong characteristics of his mother's family, one of the oldest and best in Virginia. The unselfishness, generosity, purity, and faithfulness of the Virginia Carters are widely known, and they have always been "true to all occasions true." In his mother was personified all the gentle and sweet traits of a noble woman. Her whole life was admirable, and her love for her children beyond all other thoughts. To her watchful care they were early confided by the long absence and death of her distinguished husband.

Robert was four years old when his father removed the family to Alexandria, six when he visited the West Indies for his health, and eleven when he died. If he was early trained in the way he should go, his mother trained him. If he was "always good," as his father wrote, she labored to keep him so. If his principles were sound and his life a success, to her, more than to any other, should the praise be given. . . . As Robert grew in years he grew in grace; he was like the young tree whose roots, firmly imbedded in the earth, hold it straight from the hour it was first planted till it develops into majestic proportions. With the fostering care of such a mother the son must go straight, for she had planted him in the soil of truth, morality, and religion, so that his boyhood was marked by everything that produces nobility of character in manhood. The handsome boy was studious and sedate, was popular with other boys, stood high in the estimation of his teachers, and his early inspiration was good, for his first thoughts were directed upon subjects by an excellent mother.

FITZHUGH LEE, *General Lee, pp. 20-22*

From a Soldier Father to His Sons

It is most unlikely that Robert Lee retained any direct memory of his father. When Robert was only six years old unfortunate circumstances separated them. In the early summer of 1813, Henry Lee, hopelessly in debt, unreconciled to a second war with Britain, physically crippled, and wholly dependent on the income of his wife, left home and family for the British island of Barbadoes, where he was to spend the remaining years of his life in voluntary exile. The vices of the father made no imprint on the mind of the son. To Robert, Lighthorse Harry Lee, dashing cavalry leader and hero of the Revolution, remained forever an inspiration. The precepts of this famous father addressed in "letters of love and wisdom" from the West Indies to an older son, Charles Carter Lee, were building stones in the character of his youngest son, Robert.

From Port-au-Prince, St. Domingo, June 26, 1816.

you know my abhorrence of lying, and you have been often told by me, that it led to every vice and cancelled every tendency to virtue.

From Caicos, September 30, 1816.

I would rather see you unlearned and unnoticed, if virtuous in practice as well as theory, than see you the equal in glory to the great Washington. . . .

From Nassau, New Providence, December 1, 1816.

. . . avoid all frivolous authors; such as novel writers, and all skeptical authors, whether religious, philosophic, or moral. . . .

From Nassau, February 9, 1817.

Fame in arms or art, however conspicuous, is naught, unless bottomed on virtue. . . .

It is hard to say whether too much drinking or too much eating most undermines the constitution. . . .

Cleanliness of person is not only comely to all beholders, but is indispensable to sanctity of body. Trained by your best of mothers to value it, you will never lose sight of it. . . .

Many . . . fall into another habit which hurts only themselves and which certainly stupefies the senses—immoderate sleeping. . . .

From Nassau, April 19, 1817.

The rank of men, as established by the concurrent judgment of ages, stands thus: heroes, legislators, orators, and poets. The most useful and, in my opinion, the most honorable is the legislator, which so far from being incompatible with the profession of law, is congenial to it. Generally, mankind admire most the hero; of all, the most useless, except when the safety of a nation demands his saving arm. . . .

From Nassau, May 5, 1817.

. . . self command . . . is the pivot upon which the character, fame and independence of us mortals hang. . . .

From Nassau, September 3, 1817.

Avoid debt, the sink of mental power and the subversion of independence, which draws into debasement even virtue, in appearance certainly, if not in reality. *"A man ought not only to be virtuous in reality, but he must always appear so";* thus said to me the great Washington. . . .

From New Providence, Nassau, November 20, 1817.

Admiration is not a relation of the understanding or a perception of our reason; but a sentiment of the soul, which arises in us from a certain, indescribable instinct of Deity, at sight of extraordinary objects, and from the very mysteriousness in which they are involved.

[Quoting St. Pierre] "Religion places all on a level. She humbles the head of the mighty by showing the vanity of their power, and she raises up the head of the unfortunate by disclosing the prospect of immortality. . . ."

From Nassau, January 24, 1818.

In all my letters I urge you to habits of virtue in mind and body as the only path to happiness in this life, and as the most probable security to happiness in another world. But . . . what is happiness? *Hoc opus, hic labor est.* Peace of mind based on piety to Almighty God, unconscious innocence of conduct with good will to man; health of body, health of mind, and prosperity in our vocation; a sweet, affectionate wife; *sana mens in corpore sano;* children devoted to truth, honor, right, and utility, with love and respect to their parents; and faithful and warm-hearted friends, in a country politically and religiously free;—this is my definition. . . .

Note: The foregoing excerpts were taken from letters quoted by Robert E. Lee in the biography of his father, General Henry Lee, which serves as an introduction to the third edition of the revolutionary hero's book "Memoirs of the War in the Southern Department of the United States," published in 1870, pp. 57-77.

How Can I Live Without Robert?

Robert Lee was the youngest son in a family of five children and on his shoulders very early came to rest the responsibilities which rightfully belonged to his absent father. His sister, Ann, to whom he was devoted, was delicate and required frequent medical care in Philadelphia. His oldest brother, Carter, was a student at Cambridge, and in 1819 opened a law practice in Washington, D. C., which demanded most of his time. The following year, Sidney Smith Lee accepted a midshipman's commission in the Navy. Meanwhile, Mrs. Lee, herself, was gradually slipping into chronic invalidism, and her daughter, Mildred, was too young to be of much aid in household matters.

. . . so Robert was the housekeeper, carried "the keys," attended to the marketing, managed all the out-door business, and took care of his mother's horses.

At the hour when the other school-boys went to play, he hurried home to order his mother's drive, and would then be seen carrying her in his arms to the carriage, and arranging her cushions with the gentleness of an experienced nurse. One of his relatives still lives who was often the companion of these drives. She tells us of the exertions he would make on these occasions to entertain and amuse his mother; assuring her, with the gravity of an old man, that unless she was cheerful, the drive would not benefit her. When she complained of cold or "draughts," he would pull from his pocket a great jack-knife and newspaper, and make her laugh with his efforts to improvise curtains, and shut out the intrusive wind which whistled through the crevices of the old family-coach.

When he left her to go to West Point, his mother was heard to say, "How can I live without Robert? He is both son and daughter to me."

EMILY V. MASON, *Popular Life of General Robert E. Lee, pp. 22-23.*

He Is Disposed to Devote Himself to the Profession of Arms

When Lee was seventeen, he applied for an appointment to the Military Academy. His application was made in person to the Secretary of War, John C. Calhoun, to whom he was introduced by the family counselor and kinsman, William H. Fitzhugh.

I cannot permit the young gentleman, who will hand you this letter, to make his intended application, without carrying with him, such testimony in his behalf, as a long and intimate acquaintance both with himself and his family, justify me in giving. He is the son of Genl. Henry Lee, with whose history, you are, of course, acquainted; and who (whatever may have been the misfortune of his latter years) had certainly established, by his revolutionary services, a strong claim to the gratitude of his country. He is the son also of one of the finest women, the State of Virginia has ever produced. Possessed, in a very eminent degree, of all those qualities, which peculiarly belong to the female character of the South, she is rendered doubly interesting by her meritorious & successful exertions to support, in comfort, a large family, and to give to all her children excellent educations.

The young gentleman, who I have now the pleasure of introducing to you, as a candidate for West-Point, is her youngest son. An intimate acquaintance, & a constant intercourse with him, almost from his infancy, authorize me to speak in the most unqualified terms of his amiable disposition, & his correct and gentlemanly habits. He is disposed to devote himself to the profession of arms. But his final determination on this subject, must, of course, depend on the result of his present application, and you will find him prepared to acquiesce in whatever decision, circumstances may require you to make in his case. Next, however, to promising him the commission, which he asks, the greatest favor you can do him will be to tell him promptly if you think the obstacles to his success are insurmountable. His own age (eighteen I believe) and the situation of his mother require that he lose no time in selecting the employment to which his future life is to be devoted.

FITZHUGH TO CALHOUN, *February 7, 1824.* MS National Archives.

With High Honors

Lee supplemented his application with a barrage of endorsements and testimonials from his schoolmaster, his three brothers, four representatives and five senators. These glowing endorsements which helped him win the coveted appointment were never discredited. In the Class of 1829 he was graduated with second highest honors and in his senior year he served as Adjutant of the Corps. In the four years at the Military Academy he had not received a single demerit. One of Lee's early mentors, Benjamin Hallowell, provides a clue to the success of his pupil at West Point and in all ventures he was to encounter throughout his life.

Robert E. Lee entered my school in Alexandria, Virginia, in the winter of 1824-5, to study mathematics preparatory to his going to West Point. He was a most exemplary student in every respect. He was never behind time at his studies; never failed in a single recitation; was perfectly observant of the rules and regulations of the Institution; was gentlemanly, unobtrusive, and respectful in all his deportment to teachers and fellow-students. His specialty was *finishing up*. He imparted a finish and a neatness, as he proceeded, to everything he undertook. One of the branches of mathematics he studied with me was conic sections, in which some of the diagrams are very complicated. He drew the diagrams on a slate; and although he well knew that the one he was drawing would have to be removed to make room for another, he drew each one with as much accuracy and finish, lettering and all, as if it was to be engraved and printed. . . .

BENJAMIN HALLOWELL quoted in Mason's Popular Life of General Robert E. Lee, p. 25.

The Apprenticed Engineer

An honor graduate, Lee had the privilege to choose the branch of service in which he desired to be commissioned, and at his request he was assigned to the Corps of Engineers. Home at Georgetown for a few brief weeks, he tended his mother through her last illness and had just settled the family affairs when he received his first orders.

> Engineer Order No. 8
>
> Engineer Department
> Washington, August 11, 1829
>
> Brevet 2nd Lieut. Robert E. Lee, of the Corps of Engineers, will, by the middle of November next, report to Major Sam'l Babcock for duty at Cockspur Island, in the Savannah River, Georgia.
>
> [Sgd] C. GRATIOT, *Brig. Gen. Commdg.* MS National Archives.

Fourteen miles downstream from Savannah, mosquito ridden Cockspur undoubtedly promised to be a dismal post. This small island, formed of marsh, mud, and sand, scarcely out of water at high tide, could offer but little in the way of recreation to a vigorous young man, but it is possible that no other assignment could have provided Lee with a greater variety of experience so early in his career. Due to the ill health of his senior officer, Major Babcock, he was often placed on his own responsibility and for nearly two years he was closely associated with the opening operations in the construction of the large brick fortification later to be named Fort

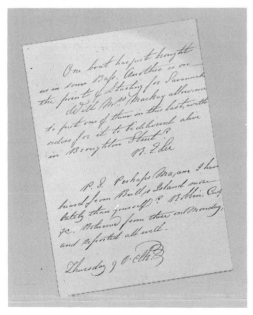

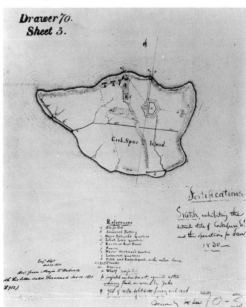

Note from *R. E. Lee to Mrs. Robert Mackay, mother of Jack Mackay, Lee's West Point chum. Undated, this note probably was written in late November, 1829, when the bass were running at Cockspur Island.*

Cockspur Island, *sketch made by Lt. R. E. Lee to show progress of work at the end of January 1830.*

5

Napoleon. *Lee made this drawing June 29, 1830, for Margaret Mackay of Savannah, Ga. This date is significant as it was the day on which Miss Mackay was married to Ralph Emms Elliott. The marriage took place in the parlor of the Mackay House on Broughton Street. Lee, who was a member of the wedding party, had a diabolic sense of humor. Why he presented so gruesome a drawing to a young lady on her wedding day may be explained when one notes that the profile of the dead hero is that of Lee, himself. From the original in the collection of Mr. Charles Mills.*

Pulaski. Babcock resigned and was replaced in command at Cockspur by Lieut. J. K. F. Mansfield, who with the help of Lee got the huge project well under way by the spring of 1831.

When not required on the job, Lee found pleasant diversion in Savannah where he met many charming people through his West Point classmate and chum, Jack Mackay. Through the gay, lighthearted notes he wrote to Mackay's sisters, Margaret, Eliza, and Catherine, he reveals for the first time his sense of humor and his joy in living which were to carry him safely through many crises in the years to come. Awaiting transfer to Fort Monroe, Virginia, Lee wrote the following farewell to Eliza and Catherine, who were then visiting in Beaufort, South Carolina, and whom he did not expect to see again before he departed.

There has been but one redeeming circumstance in the occurrences of [this] day Miss Eliza & that has been the arrival of your letter. Indeed I have been dreadfully harassed by these two men, Who call themselves Engineers. For you must known that Capt. Delafield has arrived & is in high consultation about Foundations; Grillage, Piles & what not. And I have made them more little troublesome plans & worse calculations about weight, cost, etc. of Masonry, Lime, sand & such stuff than I intend to do tomorrow, and that's the certain of it. Will you believe that they are still at it, & have just touched upon cranes, "With Lee give us a sketch of that?" But I happened to have my watch in my hand & seeing that it was ten minutes to 11 P.M. says: "Yes Capt Tomorrow" And then I takes up this table & placed it by the fire, with pen ink & paper. And I will leave them to themselves, & They shall leave us to ourselves. . . . But Miss Eliza, this parting with all in Broughton St. is dreadful. . . . Perhaps, owing to Capt. D's arrival I shall be obliged to stay longer. Perhaps, I can get to Beaufort. Perhaps your two weeks will be *out* next Tuesday, Perhaps I shall be taken sick. . . . I have not yet fixed upon the day I shall go or how. . . .

R. E. LEE TO ELIZA A. MACKAY, *April 13, 1831.*
MS in Collections of Fort Pulaski National Monument.

What a Happy Day

Before the second summer Lee was ordered from Cockspur Island to Fort Monroe, and once back in Virginia, he lost no time in laying siege to the heart of Mary Custis. The romance, begun in childhood, finally won the reluctant approval of Mary's father, George Washington Parke Custis, who was the grandson of Martha Washington and the adopted son of George Washington. Mr. Custis had no objection to Lee, himself, but was dismayed by the financial prospects of a man dependent on a military career. The gala ceremony at Arlington is described by the bride's cousin, Marietta Fauntleroy Turner Powell, who was a bridesmaid.

The night of the wedding at Arlington happened to be one of steady rain, and much fun arose from the appearance of the Rev. Mr. Ruel Keith who arrived drenched to the skin, and though a tall man was compelled to conduct the nuptial service in the clothes of my Cousin George Washington Parke Custis, a very great gentleman but a very small man, so far as inches were concerned. . . . It was the thirtieth of June, 1831—and though the mid-summer rain denied the company the enjoyment of the gardens, which command an unparalleled view of the Potomac and the City of Washington, the evening was one to be long remembered. My cousin, always a modest and affectionate girl, was never lovelier and Robert Lee with his bright eyes and high color was the picture of a cavalier. The elegance and simplicity of the bride's parents, presiding over the feast, and the happiness of the grinning servants, untainted by any disloyalty, and unreproved by their master and mistress, remain in my memory as a piece of Virginia life pleasant to recall.

MARIETTA MINNIGERODE ANDREWS, *Scraps of Paper, pp. 202-203.*

After the wedding gaieties were over, Lee wrote to his close friend and commanding officer, Andrew Talcott, of the Engineers:

So Captain, you would not come up to Arlington on that memorable Thursday. But I gave you the severest scolding you have had this many a day, from which I hope you derive great benefit. However you would have seen nothing strange, for there was neither fainting nor fighting, nor anything uncommon which could be twisted into an adventure. The Parson had few words to say, though he dwelt upon them as if he had been reading my death warrant, and there was a tremulousness in the hand I held, that made me anxious for him to end. I am told I looked "pale and interesting" which might have been the fact. But I felt as "bold as a sheep" & was surprised at my want of Romance in so great a degree as not to feel more excitement than at the Black Board at West Point. The Party all kept together till the following Tuesday, when most of them departed, particularly the Gentlemen. Some of the Ladies remained the rest of the week. And we were then left alone. I would tell you how the time passed, but fear, I am too much prejudiced to say anything more, but that it went *very* rapidly & still continues to do so. . . .

R. E. LEE TO CAPT. ANDREW J. TALCOTT, July 13, 1831, quoted from the original manuscript. Courtesy Mrs. Douglas S. Freeman, Richmond, Va.

Lee never forgot the incidents of the wedding, and at the end of June in the dark summer 1864, when the Federal forces were crowding around him at Petersburg, he found time to write his wife in remembrance of the anniversary:

Do you recollect what a happy day thirty-three years ago this was? How many hopes and pleasures it gave birth to! God has been very merciful and kind to us, and how thankless and sinful I have been. I pray that He may continue His mercies and blessings to us, and give us a little peace and rest together in this world, and finally gather us and all He has given us around His throne in the world to come. . . .

CAPTAIN ROBERT E. LEE [JR.] Recollections and Letters of General Robert E. Lee, p. 133.

Mary Custis, *wife of Robert E. Lee, from a portrait by William E. West at Baltimore, Maryland, March, 1838. Courtesy, Lee Memorial Chapel, Washington and Lee University, Lexington, Va.*

Terrapin and Alligator. *Pen and ink drawing made by R. E. Lee for Catharine Mackay, probably in April 1831. From the original in the collection of Fort Pulaski National Monument.*

I Always Knew It Was Impossible to Disobey My Father

Mildred Childe Lee

Mary Lee

Robert E. Lee, Jr.

Agnes Lee

Seven children were born to the union of Robert E. Lee and Mary Custis, three boys and four girls; George Washington Custis, 1832; Mary, 1835; William Henry Fitzhugh (Rooney), 1837; Annie Carter, 1839 Agnes, 1841; Robert Edward, Jr., 1843; and Mildred Childe, 1846. To his wife and his children Lee was passionately devoted, but the demands of his soldierly profession were to bring him many lonely periods far from home and fireside. His letters written to intimate friends and to members of his family through the years give a vivid impression of Lee as a father as he progressed from the exuberance of youth to sober maturity and at last to calm assurance through the acceptance of God's Will.

1833.

ackay My Child

. . . You told me that Miss Eliza was the mother of a little girl. . . . Do remember me most kindly to her & say to the little one, that I have a young man entirely at her service. The *modesty* which he has inherited from his *Father* forbids him from entering in person, upon so delicate a subject, but he says, without her beauty & brightness his young days will be dark & dreary, & that the Bower of roses which he has planted would be changed to a Hut of willows. . . .

R. E. LEE TO JOHN MACKAY, *January 23, 1833.*
MS Collection, Fort Pulaski, N.M.

1836. Springtime

The country looks very sweet now, and the hill at A. [Arlington] covered with verdure, and perfumed by the blossoms of the trees, the flowers of the Garden, Honey-suckles, yellow Jasmine, &c is more to my taste than at any other season of the year. But the brightest flower there blooming is my *daughter,* oh, she is a rare one, and if only sweet sixteen, I would wish myself a *cannibal,* that I might eat her up. As it is, I have given all the young ladies a holyday, and hurry home to her every day. . . .

R. E. LEE TO CAPT. ANDREW J. TALCOTT. MS., May 5, 1836
Talcott MSS., Virginia Historical Society.

1837. Fall

Mackay I am the father of three children, and you are but a leafless bough. They are whole children Mackay, and so entwined around my heart, that I feel them at every pulsation. You say right, life is too short for them and their mother to be in one place, and I in another. I am hurrying back with all dispatch.

R. E. LEE TO JOHN MACKAY, *October 22, 1837,* FRANK B. SCREVEN,
"Letters of R. E. Lee to the Mackay Family."

1839. Enroute to St. Louis

You do not know how much I have missed you and the children, my dear Mary. To be alone in a crowd is very solitary. In the woods I feel sympathy with the trees and birds, in whose company I take delight, but experience no pleasure in a strange crowd.

I hope you are all well and will continue so, and therefore must again urge you to be prudent and careful of those dear children. If I could only get a squeeze at that little fellow turning up his sweet mouth to "keese baba!" You must not let him run wild in my absence, and will have to exercise firm authority over all of them. This will not require severity,

8

Robert E. Lee, Jr.

Mildred Childe Lee

or even strictness, but constant attention and an unwavering course. Mildness and forbearance, temperance by firmness and judgment, will strengthen their affection for you, while it will maintain your control over them.

> R. E. Lee to Mrs. Lee, *June 5, 1839*, J. William Jones,
> *Personal Reminiscences, Anecdotes, and Letters of Gen. Robert E. Lee, p. 369.*

1839. Harvest Time

My dearest Jack

... Do you know how many little Lees there are now? It is astonishing with what facility the precious creatures are dressed up for the return of their Papas! I am sure to be introduced to a new one every Christmas. They are the dearest annuals of the season, and I find something in every edition that I in vain look for elsewhere. I am informed that there is now at home a little long nosed fellow for my first benediction, and my sister Nanie, has a black headed duplicate to greet the arrival of my sailor brother from the West Indies. With what a bountiful hand are these little responsibilities distributed.

> R. E. Lee to John Mackay, *November 8, 1839.* Frank B. Screven,
> *"Letters of R. E. Lee to the Mackay Family."*

Gen. William Henry Fitzhugh "Rooney" Lee

1848. Home from Mexico

Here I am once again, my dear Smith, perfectly surrounded by Mary and her precious children, who seem to devote themselves to staring at the furrows in my face and the white hairs in my head. It is not surprising that I am hardly recognisable to some of the young eyes around me and perfectly unknown to the youngest. But some of the older ones gaze with astonishment and wonder at me, and seem at a loss to reconcile what they see and what was pictured in their imaginations. I find them, too, much grown, and all well, and I have much cause for thankfulness, and gratitude to that good God who has once more united us.

> R. E. Lee to His Brother, Smith Lee, *June 30, 1848.*
> R. E. Lee [Jr.], *Recollections and Letters, p. 4.*

Gen. George Washington Custis Lee

1851. To his oldest son at West Point

The full play of your young and growing powers, the daily exercise of all your energies, the consciousness of acquiring knowledge, and the pleasure of knowing your efforts to do your duty, will bring you a delight and justification far surpassing all that idleness and selfishness can give. Try it fairly and take your own experience. ... Hold yourself above every mean action. Be strictly honorable in every act, and be not ashamed to *do right*. Acknowledge right to be your aim and strive to reach it. . . .

R. E. LEE TO G. W. C. LEE, Baltimore, *May 4, 1851.* Quoted in J. William Jones
Life and Letters of Robert Edward Lee, Soldier and Man, p. 72.

1852.   To his son, Custis

You must study to be frank with the world. Frankness is the child of honesty and courage. Say just what you mean to do on every occasion, and take it for granted you mean to do right. . . . Never do a wrong thing to make a friend or to keep one. . . . Above all, do not appear to others what you are not. . . . We should live, act, and say nothing to the injury of anyone. . . .

R. E. LEE TO G. W. C. LEE, Arlington, *April 5, 1852.*
Quoted in *Lee of Virginia* by EDMUND JENNINGS LEE, *pp. 432-433.*

1853.   Advice from West Point to his daughters

My Precious Annie . . . I hope you will always appear to me as you are now painted on my heart, and that you will endeavour to improve and so conduct yourself as to make you happy and me joyful all our lives. Diligent and earnest attention to *all* your duties can only accomplish this. I am told you are growing very tall, and I hope very straight. I do not know what the Cadets will say if the Superintendent's *children* do not practice what he demands of them. They will naturally say he had better attend to his own before he corrects other people's children, and as he permits his to stoop, it is hard he will not allow them. You and Agnes must not, therefore, bring me into discredit with my young friends, or give them reason to think that I require more of them than of my own. . . .

R. E. LEE TO HIS DAUGHTER, West Point, *February 25, 1853.*
R. E. LEE [JR.], *Recollections and Letters, pp. 14-15.*

Fifty years later, Robert E. Lee, Jr., had this memory of his father.

He was always bright and gay with us little folk, romping, playing, and joking with us. With the older children, he was just as companionable, and I have seen him join my elder brothers and their friends when they would try their powers at a high jump put up in our yard. The two younger children he petted a great deal, and our greatest treat was to get into his bed in the morning and lie close to him, listening while he talked to us in his bright, entertaining way. This custom we kept up until I was ten years old and over. Although he was so joyous and familiar with us, he was very firm on all proper occasions, never indulged us in anything that was not good for us, and exacted the most implicit obedience. I always knew that it was impossible to disobey my father. I felt it in me, I never thought why, but was perfectly sure when he gave an order that it had to be obeyed. . . .

R. E. LEE [JR.], *Recollections and Letters, p. 9.*

Two Bottles of Brandy

Lee was endowed with a magnificent physique which he maintained by regular exercise and orderly living. He seldom condemned others for weakness of character, but for himself he did not willingly permit such weaknesses. Wrote Chaplain Jones:

He was exceedingly abstemious in his own habits. He never used tobacco, and rarely took even a single glass of wine. Whiskey or brandy he did not drink, and he did all in his power to discourage their use by others.

In the spring of 1861, while on an inspection tour to Norfolk, a friend there insisted that he should take two bottles of very fine old "London Dock" brandy, remarking that he would be certain to need it, and would find it very difficult to obtain so good an article. General Lee declined the offer, saying that he was sure he would not need it. "As proof that I will not," he said, "I may tell you that, just as I was starting to the Mexican War, a lady in Virginia prevailed on me to take a bottle of fine old whiskey, which she thought I could not get on without. I carried that bottle all through the war without having had the slightest occasion to use it, and on my return home I sent it back to my good friend, that she might be convinced that I could get on without liquor."

But the gentleman still insisted, and the general politely yielded and took the two bottles.

At the close of the war he met a brother of this gentleman (from whom I get the incident) in Lexington, and said to him: "Tell your brother that I kept the brandy he gave me all through the war, and should have it yet, but that I was obliged to use it last summer in a severe illness of one of my daughters."

During the war he was accustomed to do everything in his power, both by precept and example, to prevent drunkenness among his officers and men, and more than once he refused to promote an officer who drank too freely, saying, "I cannot consent to place in the control of others one who cannot control himself."

JONES, Personal Reminiscences of General Robert E. Lee, p. 169-170.

To the end of his life Lee never lost his deep concern for the well-being of his children. He set a high moral standard for himself and he was satisfied with nothing less for his sons and daughters. This concern is well illustrated in advice he wrote to his son, "Rooney" when that young man went west to join his cavalry command.

I hope you will always be distinguished for your avoidance of the "universal balm," *whiskey*, and every immorality. Nor need you fear to be ruled out of the society that indulges in it, for you will acquire their esteem and respect, as all venerate if they do not practice virtue. I am sorry to say that there is great proclivity for spirit in the army in the field. It seems to be considered a substitute for every luxury. The great body may not carry it to extremes, but many pursue it to their ruin. With some it is used as a means of hospitality. . . . I think it better to avoid it altogether, as you do, as its temperate use is so difficult. I hope you will make many friends, as you will be thrown with those who deserve this feeling, but indiscriminate intimacies you will find annoying and entangling, and they can be avoided by politeness and civility. You see I am following my old habit of giving advice, which I dare say you neither need nor require. But you must pardon a fault which proceeds from my great love and burning anxiety for your welfare and happiness. When I think of your youth, impulsiveness, and many temptations, your distance from me, and the ease (and even innocence) with which you might commence an erroneous course, my heart quails within me, and my whole frame and being tremble at the possible result. May Almighty God have you in His holy keeping! To His merciful providence I commit you, and will rely upon Him, and the efficacy of the prayers that will be daily and hourly offered up by those who love you.

R. E. LEE TO W. H. F. LEE, May 30, 1858, JONES,
Personal Reminiscences of General Robert E. Lee, pp. 376-377.

Advice on Smoking:

I was sorry to see, from your letter to your mother, that you smoke occasionally. It is dangerous to meddle with. You have in store so much better employment for your mouth. Reserve it, Roon, for its legitimate pleasure. Do not poison and corrupt it with stale vapors, or tarnish your beard with their stench. . . .

R. E. LEE TO W. H. F. LEE, January 1, 1859, JONES,
Personal Reminiscences of General Robert E. Lee.

He Is Not at All High Church

Robert E. Lee was born of an Episcopalian mother who made sure that her son formed the habit of attending church regularly. She taught him also to commune with God daily through prayer. Yet, notwithstanding his regularity in public and private worship, Lee did not become a member of any church until he was 46 years old. In 1853 he offered himself and his daughters for confirmation at Christ Church, Alexandria. Robert E. Lee, Jr. described his father during this period when he was Superintendent at West Point.

My father was the most punctual man I ever knew. He was always ready for family prayers, for meals, and met every engagement, social or business, at the moment. He expected all of us to be the same, and taught the use and necessity of forming such habits for the convenience of all concerned. I never knew him late for Sunday service at the Post Chapel. He used to appear some minutes before the rest of us, in uniform, jokingly rallying my mother for being late, and for forgetting something at the last moment. When he could wait no longer for her, he would say that he was off and would march along to church by himself, or with any of the children who were ready. There he sat very straight—well up the middle aisle—and, as I remember, always became very sleepy, and sometimes even took a little nap during the sermon. At that time, this drowsiness of my father's was something awful to me, inexplicable. I knew it was very hard for me to keep awake, and frequently I did not; but why he, who to my mind could do everything that was right, without any effort, should sometimes be overcome, I could not understand, and did not try to do so.

R. E. LEE, [JR.], *Recollections and Letters, p. 12.*

Lee may have dozed through a few sermons, but he was never far from God, who to him was a very personal deity. From the time of the Mexican War onward, his correspondence showed that he was growing steadily in religious consciousness. In the midstream of the Civil War he exerted over the men under him the power of a great evangelist. After the Battle of Gettysburg, his order requiring the observance of a fast day appointed by President Davis had a profound effect.

General Order No. 83
Headquarters Army Northern Virginia, August 13, 1863

The President of the Confederate States has, in the name of the people, appointed the 21st day of August as a day of fasting, humiliation, and prayer. A strict observance of the day is enjoined upon the officers and soldiers of this army. All military duties, except such as are absolutely necessary, will be suspended. The commanding officers of brigades and regiments are requested to cause divine services, suitable to the occasion, to be performed in their respective commands.

Soldiers! We have sinned against Almighty God. We have forgotten his signal mercies, and have cultivated a revengeful, haughty, and boastful spirit. We have not remembered that the defenders of a just cause should be pure in his eyes; that "our times are in his hands;" and we have relied too much on our own arms for the achievement of our independence. God is our only refuge and our strength. Let us humble ourselves before him. Let us confess our many sins, and beseech Him to give us a higher courage, a purer patriotism, and more determined will; that He will convert the hearts of our enemies; that He will hasten the time when war, with its sorrows and sufferings, shall cease, and that He will give us a name and place among the nations of the earth.

R. E. LEE, *General.*

Wrote Chaplain Jones:

We can never forget the effect produced by the reading of this order at the solemn services of that memorable fast day. A precious revival was already in progress in many of the commands. The day was almost universally observed; the attendance upon preaching and other services was very large; the solemn attention and starting tear attested the deep interest felt; and the work of grace among the troops widened and deepened, and went gloriously on until there had been at least *fifteen thousand* professions of faith in Christ as a personal Saviour. How far these grand results were due to this fast-day, or to the quiet influence and fervent prayers of the commanding general, eternity alone shall reveal.

JONES, *Personal Reminiscences of General Robert E. Lee, pp. 421-422.*

In the last months of his life when Lee journeyed southward for his health an old friend in Savannah said of him:

I think he is altogether of the highest type of mankind & his nobility of soul struck me continually as well as his profound sense of religion he is not at all high church & when somebody spoke about the observance of lent he said "If you will only fast from your sins you may *eat* what you please. . . ."

MARGARET COWPER MACKAY ELLIOTT TO LUCY TROWBRIDGE,
April, 1870; MS courtesy Miss Clermont Lee, Savannah, Ga.

Steamboat, "Yellow Stone," *leaving St. Louis, site of Lee's first major engineering job. From a painting by George Catlin made in the 1830's. In the Collections of the Smithsonian Institution.*

Not Unmindful of the Future

When Lee was about 30 years of age, he became seriously interested in a study of his ancestors and wrote to his cousin, Cassius Lee for a history of the Lee family and a copy of the coat-of-arms. The motto of the Lee Arms is "Non Incautus Futuri" (not unmindful of the future).

It is possible that at this time Lee may have formulated the code on which he patterned his life and from which he never deviated. This amazing code, written in his own autograph on a scrap of paper, was found in his military valise after his death.

The forebearing use of power does not only form a touchstone, but the manner in which an individual enjoys certain advantages over others is a test of a *true gentleman.*

The power which the strong have over the weak, the magistrate over the citizen, the employer over the employed, the educated over the unlettered, the experienced over the confiding, even the clever over the silly—the forbearing or inoffensive use of all this power or authority, or a total abstinence from it when the case admits it, will show the gentleman in a plain light. The gentleman does not needlessly and unnecessarily remind an offender of a wrong he may have committed against him. He cannot only forgive, he can forget; and he strives for that nobleness of self and mildness of character which impart sufficient strength to let the past be but the past. *A true man of honor feels humbled himself when he cannot help humbling others.*

JONES, Personal Reminiscences of General Robert E. Lee, p. 163.

This Is a Beautiful Country

Lee's military assignments carried him far and wide across the continent of North America and tended to inculcate in him a much broader concept of the nation than would be possible in an ordinary private citizen. At one time or another, he inspected the whole Atlantic Coast from New England to Florida. He traveled to the Great Lakes, the middle west along the Mississippi and the Missouri, through the great plains to the far corners of Texas, and to the Gulf of Mexico. He loved America, as his letters to friends and relatives so eloquently reveal.

The Upper Mississippi, 1837.

This is a beautiful country, and one day must be a great one. The soil is so fertile, trees so grand, and verdure so rich. I allude principally to the upper Mississippi. The people are rough, but they will polish and as soon as they relinquish laying off towns— and instead of magnificent cities on paper, raise wheat and corn on the land, they will begin to thrive.

"The prairies are enveloped in flames and smoke"—the country west of the Mississippi so eloquently described by Lee.

From a painting *by George Catlin in the Collections of the Smithsonian Institution. Plate, courtesy of the Dial Press, New York City.*

There are quite some pretty and flourishing villages, however, now on the river, and when you consider that it has been only three years since the greater part of them were founded, you will allow the inhabitants do deserve some credit. There will be less of these in ten years. Some will decay and others will grow apace. If you can help me distinguish these last, I can help you to make a fortune.

R. E. LEE TO LT. JOHN MACKAY, *October 22, 1837*, F. B. SCREVEN,
"The Letters of R. E. Lee to the Mackay Family."

West of the Mississippi, 1838.

. . . Everything gives token of an early approach of winter. Flocks of geese and brant are continually passing over us in their flight South. The trees present a dreary appearance, and the prairies are enveloped in flames and smoke. Night before last there was ice strong enough, in the language of the natives, "to bear a dog"! And we yesterday had a charming snowstorm which in the night changed to rain, and we were this morning greeted with a beautiful sight.

We are fixed at the house at a neat Yankee couple on the banks of the Miss., which with the stable and their house compose the city of Montebello. Our hostess is quite a nice cook, and we have now hanging in her larder in the way of game (I speak from an inspection this morning) 13 prairie hens, one plover blue wing, 2 red-headed woodpeckers and a squirrel. Besides practicing in this art, she has to do all the work about the house, wash, sew, and mind her child, who is just learning to walk. In a word she and her husband do everything that is required about the house and farm. Would it not make you nervous to see a woman work so? She is quite a well educated and delicate young woman. Her center table is furnished with an album, prints, etc., and her shelves with Sterne, Byron, and so on. There are three boarders besides ourselves, with an occasional passenger or two, who eat up all the pumpkin pies as fast as she can make them.

. . . Mackay, if you were here, you would certainly kill yourself. Why, man, in half an hour you can put up 200 prairie hens, and have a prairie 60 miles in extent to shoot them in. As to partridges you can hardly keep from stumbling over them and hares and squirrels are out of number.

There are abundance of woodcocks, in season, and some pheasants, and the river is now getting covered with ducks. Turkeys and deer are to be had for walking after and you may fish from years end to years end.

R. E. LEE TO CAPT. JOHN MACKAY, *October 19, 1838*, F. B. SCREVEN,
"The Letters of R. E. Lee to the Mackay Family."

New York, 1846.

We had a very deep snow some 10 or 12 days ago, over 10 inches on a level, followed by severe cold and high Northwesters for two or three days. This banked up the snow in parts of the roads higher than the fences and during the continuance of the wind rendered them almost impassable. After it subsided, it required 2 or 3 days to open the roads, which had to be done by excavating with shovels. Then we had fine sleighing . . . it was a joyous time while the sleighing lasted, and you may depend it was made the most of. Day and night the bells were going. And those bitter cold nights the young women kept it up till 10 and 12 o'clock. During its height I went up Broadway to witness it. There was not a wheel carriage to be seen, but a rushing stream of sleighs of all sizes and descriptions flying in both directions. The corners of all cross streets into B. W. were crowded with spectators. The men hurrahing, the women laughing and the boys screaming with delight. There were some beautiful turn outs of sleighs and horses. I have never seen such fine horses in N. Y. and the variety of the sleighs and richness of the furs were beyond my anticipation. But the ladies with their smiling faces and gay dresses exceeded all. Some of the omnibus sleighs were very large. I was in one that carried 50 people. It was drawn by 8 horses. There were many of this size, and one belonging to the same line carried 75. Kip & Brown I was told was building one, to be out the next day, that would carry 250. There was one called the Oregon, drawn by 18 horses, all driven in hand by one man on a seat about

10 ft. above them and on a platform behind him was a full band of music. I did not learn how many passengers it carried. But they went "the whole or none." The girls returning from school were the prettiest sight; piled on each others laps with their bags of books and laughing faces. Indeed there were no lack of customers at sixpence a ride, and you might be accommodated with a lady in your lap in the bargain. Think of a man of my forbiding countenance John Mackay having such an offer. But I peeped under her veil before accepting, and though I really could not find fault either with her appearance or age, after a little demurring preferred giving her my seat. I thought it would not sound well if repeated in the latitude of Washington that I had been riding down B. W. with a strange woman on my lap. . . .

R. E. LEE TO CAPT. JOHN MACKAY, Fort Hamilton, N. Y., *January 30, 1846.*
Typescript in Collection of Fort Pulaski National Monument.

II. CROWNED WITH HONORS

Opportunity first knocked at the door of Robert E. Lee when Congress declared war on Mexico, May 13, 1846. It was twenty-one years after Lee had entered the Military Academy. Meanwhile, he had performed responsible duties in the planning and construction of fortifications. He had proved his engineering skill in the development of river and harbor works. He had shown that he could supervise the labor of large numbers of men, deal successfully with the public, and he had served on various missions under the Chief of Engineers in Washington, but up to this time he had had no practical experience as a soldier.

On August 19, 1846, Captain Lee was ordered to report for war time duty in Mexico. Here for several months he was engaged in engineering and reconnaissance work for General Wool, whose forces had crossed the Rio Grande and were advancing unopposed into the state of Chihuahua. Then came one of the luckiest breaks in his career. He was transferred to the staff of Major General Scott, who was to make the main invasion of Mexico. From this campaign on which he was about to embark, Lee was to return, in the words of Jefferson Davis, "crowned with honors, covered by brevets, and recognized, young as he was, as one of the ablest of his country's soldiers."

About the last of February, [1847], General Scott embarked his troops and sailed for Vera Cruz, and on the 9th of March landed his army of 12,000 men a short distance south of that city, which he immediately proceeded to invest. The city was surrounded by a wall and defended by a powerful fortress, the castle of San Juan de Ulloa, the number of guns being about 400. It was garrisoned by 5,000 Mexican troops under General Morales.

The establishment of batteries and the other details of the siege were directed by Captain Lee, who prosecuted his labors with such vigor that by the 22nd the batteries were ready to commence the bombardment which resulted on the 29th in the surrender of Vera Cruz and the adjacent fortifications. For his services on this occasion Captain Lee was favorably mentioned by General Scott in his report of the siege of Vera Cruz. Having gained a secure base of operations, General Scott advanced toward the city of Mexico; but on reaching Cerro Gordo, the point where the National Road emerges from the Tierra Caliente, he found himself confronted by General Santa Anna with a numerous army, which this general had, in spite of his defeat at Buena Vista, thoroughly reorganized and put in position to oppose Scott's advance.

Cerro Gordo was of such formidable strength that a direct attack was deemed injudicious, and therefore it became necessary to adopt other means for its reduction. In the words of General Scott, "Reconnoissances were pushed in search of some practicable route other than the winding, zigzag road among the spurs of mountains, with heavy batteries at every turn. The reconnoissances were conducted with vigor under Captain Lee at the head of a body of pioneers, and at the end of the third day a passable way for light batteries was accomplished without alarming the enemy, giving the possibility of turning the extreme left of his line of defense and capturing his whole army, except the reserve, that lay a mile or two higher up the road. Santa Anna said that he had not believed a goat could have approached him in that direction. Hence the surprise and the results were the greater."

A large force was sent along the route thus made passable, and, though it was discovered by the enemy before it had quite reached the point desired, it had gained a position which enabled it to storm and carry the heights of Cerro Gordo and rout the Mexican army, Santa Anna being defeated and forced to retire with great loss. General Scott, in his report of this battle says:

"I am compelled to make special mention of Captain R. E. Lee, Engineer. This officer was again indefatigable during these operations in reconnoissances as daring as laborious, and of the utmost value. Nor was he less conspicuous in planting batteries and in conducting columns to their stations under the heavy fire of the enemy."

An interesting incident which occurred during one of the reconnoissances mentioned by General Scott was related to the writer by John Fitzwalter, who acted as a guide to Captain Lee during this campaign, and who himself was so daring as to gain from the Mexicans the title of Juan Diablo, or, to put it in plain English, John the Devil.

During the reconnoissances in question Captain Lee had ventured too far from his supporting column, and unexpectedly found himself in the midst of the enemy and in a position of great danger. He was forced to take refuge beneath a fallen tree, near which was a spring to which Mexicans frequently came for water. While he lay hidden in this perilous covert hostile soldiers frequently passed over the tree, and even sat down on it and entered into conversation, without discovering the somewhat nervous individual beneath it. He was obliged to remain there until the coming of night enabled him to retire from the dangerous locality.

A. L. Long, *Memoirs of Robert E. Lee, pp. 51-53.*

Throughout the entire drive from the Gulf to Mexico City, Lee's work in reconnaissance was extraordinary and the valor he demonstrated on many occasions was beyond the call of duty. From the first moment under fire at Vera Cruz he showed remarkable coolness in situations of danger, and at Cerro Gordo, for the first time he learned the hideous quality of warfare. After the battle he wrote to his wife.

During all that night we were at work in constructing the battery, getting up the guns, ammunition, etc., and they in strengthening their defenses on Cerro Gordo. Soon after sunrise our batteries opened, and I started with a column to turn their left and to get on the Jalapa road. Notwithstanding their efforts to prevent us in this, we were perfectly successful, and the working party, following our footsteps, cut out the road for the artillery. In the meantime our storming party had reached the crest of Cerro Gordo, and seeing their whole left turned and the position of our soldiers on the Jalapa road, they broke and fled. Those in the pass laid down their arms. . . . All their cannon, arms, ammunition, and most of their men fell into our hands. The papers cannot tell you what a horrible sight a field of battle is, nor will I. . . .

In the same letter Lee showed that even in the heat of battle he was not unaware of the beauty of nature around him and that later with joyous heart he could remember what he saw.

Jalapa is the most beautiful country I have seen in Mexico, and will compare with any I have seen elsewhere. I wish it was in the United States, and that I was located with you and the children around me in one of its rich, bright valleys. I can conceive nothing more beautiful in the way of landscape or mountain scenery. We ascended upwards of four thousand feet that morning, and whenever we looked back the rich valley was glittering in the morning sun and the light morning clouds flitting around us. On reaching the top, the valley appeared at intervals between the clouds which were below us, and high over all towered Orizaba, with its silver cap of snow.

JONES, Life and Letters, pp. 51-52.

From Cerro Gordo to the capital of Mexico, Captain Lee at every point increased the reputation he was acquiring. At Contreras, Churubusco, Molino del Rey, and Chapultepec he was constantly in the saddle, performing with alacrity and courage the duties of a trusted staff officer. "Before the battle of Contreras," wrote one of the most distinguished soldiers of that war, "General Scott's troops had become separated in the field of Pedrigal, and it was necessary to communicate instruction to those on the other side of his barrier of rocks and lava. General Scott says in his report that he had sent seven officers since about sundown to communicate instructions; they had all returned without getting through, but the gallant and indefatigable Captain Lee, of the engineers, who has been constantly with the operating forces, is just in from Shields, Smith, Cadwalader, etc. . . . ."

Subsequently Scott, while giving testimony before a court of inquiry, said: "Captain Lee, of the engineers, came to me from Contreras with a message from Brigadier-General Smith. I think about the same time (midnight) he, having passed over the difficult ground by daylight, found it just possible to return on foot and alone to St. Augustine in the dark, the greatest feat of physical and moral courage performed by any individual to my knowledge, pending the campaign."

His deeds of personal daring, his scientific counsels, his *coup d'oeil* of the battlefield, his close personal reconnoissances under the scorching rays of a tropical sun, amid the lightening's flash or thunder's roar, did much to mold the key which unlocked the gates of the Golden City. The reports of his commander are filled with commendations of his bravery: "That he was as famous for felicitous execution as for science and daring;" that at "Chapultepec Captain Lee was constantly conspicuous, bearing important orders" from him "till he fainted from a wound and the loss of two nights' sleep at the batteries." This veteran general, in referring afterward to this campaign, was heard to say "that his success in Mexico was largely due to the skill, valor, and undaunted courage of Robert E. Lee. . . ."

FITZHUGH LEE, General Lee, pp. 41-42.

These brilliant services were not left without that recognition which is most dear to the heart of a soldier. Lee was steadily promoted. His gallant conduct at Cerro Gordo brought him the brevet rank of major; his services at Contreras and Churubusco brought him the additional brevet of lieutenant-colonel; and after Chapultepec he was nominated for the brevet rank of colonel—distinctions fully earned by his skill and valor.

The victory last mentioned was immediately followed by the capture of the forts which guarded the roads leading into the city and the occupation of the Mexican capital. This virtually ended the war. There was some guerilla warfare, but no battles of importance, after this achievement, the Mexicans giving up the contest as hopeless.

LONG, Memoirs of Robert E. Lee, p. 61.

School for Soldiers

In Scott's army in Mexico at that time were many subordinate officers fighting under a common flag, who were destined to become familiar to the public fourteen years afterward by the skill and courage with which they fought each other. Their swords, then drawn for victory against a common foe, were to be pointed against each other's breasts, and those who had slept beneath the same blanket, drank from the same canteen, and formed those ties of steel which are strongest when pledged amid common dangers around a common mess table, were to be marshalled under the banners of opposing armies. Ulysses S. Grant was then twenty-five years old, a lieutenant of the Fourth Infantry, self-reliant, brave, and fertile in resources. He fought with old "Zach" at Palo Alto, Resaca de la Palma, and at Monterey; was at Vera Cruz, and in all the battles which followed until the Mexican capital was entered. George Gordon Meade was an officer of topographical engineers, first on the staff of General Taylor and afterward on the staff of General Patterson at Vera Cruz. There too was George B. McClellan, twenty-one years old, as an engineer officer, who received brevets as first lieutenant and captain for his bravery in battle. Irvin McDowell, who afterward became first commander of the Army of the Potomac, was aid-de-camp to General John E. Wool. George H. Thomas was second lieutenant, Third Artillery, and was brevetted three times for gallantry; Joseph Hooker was assistant adjutant general on the staff of General Purcifor [Persifor] F. Smith; Gideon J. Pillow was brevetted three times. Ambrose E. Burnside joined the army on its march, with some recruits. Winfield Scott Hancock was there as second lieutenant, Sixth Infantry, twenty-three years of age, and was brevetted for his conduct at Contreras and Churubusco. There too was Albert Sidney Johnston of the First (Texas) Rifles and afterward inspector general of Butler's division; so also Joseph E. Johnston, lieutenant colonel of voltigeurs, wounded twice and brevetted three times. Braxton Bragg was present as a captain of a light battery in the Third Artillery, the first man to plant the regimental colors on the rampart of Chapultepec; and there too was Thomas Jonathan Jackson, twenty-three years old, second lieutenant of Magruder's light battery of artillery. Young in years and rank, he gave early evidence of those qualities of a soldier for which he became distinguished under the name of Stonewall Jackson. Magruder, his captain, commended him highly in his report, writing that "if devotion, industry, talent, and gallantry are the highest qualities of a soldier, then Lieutenant Jackson is entitled to the distinction which their possession confers." In the army also was [James] Longstreet, lieutenant of infantry twenty-six years old, brevetted twice and wounded at Chapultepec; and Magruder, known among his comrades as "Prince John," from courtly manners, distinguished appearance, and fine conversational powers, who commanded a light battery in Pillow's division, was twice brevetted and wounded at Chapultepec. John Sedgwick was with the army, first lieutenant of artillery, a classmate of Bragg and Early and Hooker, twice brevetted; and so was Richard S. Ewell, a typical dragoon; Ambrose P. Hill, only twenty-one years old, second lieutenant of the First Artillery; and Daniel H. Hill, Jubal Early, and many others who afterward became famous. Little did these young fellows, who marched, bivouacked, fought, and bled side by side on the burning sands of old Mexico, imagine that in less than two decades McDowell would be training his guns on Johnston and Beauregard at first Manassas, while McClellan, Pope, Burnside, Hooker, Meade, and Grant would each in turn test the prowess of Lee; nor did their old commander, Scott, dream he was training these young men in practical strategy, grand tactics, and the science of war, in order that they might direct the information thus acquired against each other.

After the Treaty of Peace with Mexico, Lee was assigned to the important duty of constructing works for the defense of the harbor of Baltimore, and was so occupied until 1852, when he was made Superintendent of the United States Military Academy, from whose walls he had emerged as a cadet twenty-three years before. At West Point he was employed for three years in watching over the drill, discipline, and studies of cadets, who were one day to become officers of the army. The detail was a complimentary one, and the office of superintendent at that time, by law, could only be filled by engineer officers. His accustomed ability was displayed in these new duties, and the Academy received great benefit from a sagacious administration of its affairs. . . .

FITZHUGH LEE, *General Lee*, pp. 46-51.

There Is No Rest for the Wicked

Lee's term of office at West Point was ended by his assignment to cavalry. In the spring of 1855 he was promoted to the rank of lieutenant-colonel in the newly established second cavalry under the command of Colonel Albert Sidney Johnston. It was with regret that Lee left the Engineer Corps, for there he had a national reputation, but promotion and the love of horses, no doubt, helped lessen his disappointment on being transferred from staff to line. If he gained little from his experiences in the cavalry, life in the saddle seasoned him for the strenuous ordeal he was to face in the years to come.

Except for one long furlough at Arlington, when he returned to settle the estate of his father-in-law, he spent most of his years in the cavalry on the far frontier of Texas assisting in the task of civilizing the Indians. From Arlington in 1859 he was summoned by the Secretary of War for brief duty at Harper's Ferry to suppress the so-called raid of John Brown and his companions.

From a camp on the Clear Fork of the Brazos River in Indian Territory, the 24th of May, 1856, Lee wrote to his lifelong friend, Eliza Mackay Stiles.

We are on the best of terms with our neighbors, the Camanches, & I am happy to believe that there is no love lost between us. I see more of them than I desire, & when I can be of no service take little interest in them. I was called upon the other day to visit Ila-tem-a-se, the head Chief of the Southern Camanches, who was reported quite sick & wanted a big *medicine man.* His lodges are only 2 miles below us, & when I presented myself before them on my big horse Bald Eagle, attended by an orderly dragoon, the explosion among the curs, children & women, was tremendous. The medicine men rushed at me, made significant signs that I must disrobe before presenting myself before the august patient. I patiently sat on my horse till I ascertained what garment they considered most inimical to the practice of the healing art, which I learned to be the cravat. Then alighting, unbuttoning my coat & slipping off the noxious article, I displayed to their admiring eyes

Comanche Village in Texas. *From a painting by George Catlin in the Collections of the Smithsonian Institution. The years Lee spent civilizing the Comanches gave him experience in cavalry movements and toughened his body.*

a blue check shirt, & was greeted by a general approving *humph*. The charm was fully developed, & I walked boldly in. The lodge was carpeted with Buffaloe robes. The sick man was stretched on his couch with his wives & servitors around him. His shield, bow & quiver were suspended on the outside, near which stood his favorite horse ready to be slain, to bear the spirit of his master to the far hunting ground. I thought him labouring under an attack of pleurisy—administered a loaf of bread & some sugar, of which I knew him to be very fond & which I had carried with me, & told him, I would send a man to complete his cure. So in the evg the Dr. rode down with his steward & drugs & cupped him pretty freely, which I hope will restore him. Perhaps the lancet has only reserved to the bullet the task of despatching him.

I have 4 Companies of the 2 Cavy. with me & hope to get to the Canadian during the summer. The country is fertile & rolling, lightly timbered, & the deer & antelope luxuriate in the abundant grass. We are far beyond civilization. San Antonio, 400 miles to the South, is our nearest depot. Men & horses have therefore mainly to rely upon the products of the field. You are ignorant of the luxurious salad, made of lambs quarter & young poke....

R. E. LEE TO MRS. WILLIAM HENRY STILES, *May 24, 1856.* MS. Robert E. Lee Memorial Foundation, Inc., Stratford Hall Plantation, Va.

In a postscript to a second letter addressed to Mrs. Stiles from Camp Cooper, Texas, August, 14, 1856, Lee complains:

A courier has just placed in my hands orders to go over to the Rio Grande, as far down as Comorgo—almost the furthest point in the Dept. they could send me. Truly there is no rest for the wicked.

R. E. LEE TO MRS. WILLIAM HENRY STILES, *August 14, 1856,* F. B. SCREVEN, *"The Letters of R. E. Lee to the Mackay Family."*

Slavery Is a Moral and Political Evil

As the 19th Century reached and passed the mid point the question of slavery tended more and more to become the leading political problem. This question had the specific power to inflame the passions of men, and due to the north-south distribution of free and slave states, attempts to solve the difficult problems through compromise led to sectional hostility.

Lee had no liking for slavery, and the half dozen slaves he owned were probably received as gifts from his father-in-law. In his will written in 1846, he directed that those few servants should be freed as soon after his death as could be done to their advantage. He believed in gradual emancipation, but aside from sending those of his servants to Liberia who wished to go, he made no effort toward the abolition of the system. From the day he left Fort Pulaski in 1831 until he went to Texas in 1856, he had spent very little time in any state south of Virginia, and, in consequence, had observed slavery only at its best. He shared the conviction, held by many religious people in the border states, that slavery as an institution existed by God's will, and that it would cease to exist when God so ruled. In a letter from Texas, to Mrs. Lee, he expressed his views.

 . . . In this enlightened age there are few, I believe, but will acknowledge that slavery as an institution is a moral and political evil in in any country. It is useless to expatiate on its disadvantages. I think it, however, a greater evil to the white than to the black race, and while my feelings are strongly interested in behalf of the latter, my sympathies are stronger for the former. The blacks are immeasurably better off here than in

22

Africa, morally, socially and physically. The painful discipline they are undergoing is necessary for their instruction as a race, and I hope, will prepare and lead them to better things. How long their subjection may be necessary is known and ordered by a wise and merciful Providence. Their emancipation will sooner result from a mild and melting influence than the storms and contests of fiery controversy. This influence, though slow, is sure.

The doctrines and miracles of our Saviour have required nearly two thousand years to convert but a small part of the human race, and even among Christian nations what gross errors still exist! While we see the course of the final abolition of slavery is onward, and we give it the aid of our prayers, and all justifiable means in our power, we must leave the progress as well as the result in His hands who sees the end and who chooses to work by slow things, and with whom a thousand years are but as a single day; although the abolitionist must know this ,and must see that he has neither the right nor power of operating except by moral means and suasion; and if he means well to the slave, he must not create angry feelings in the master. That although he may not approve the mode by which it pleases Providence to accomplish its purposes, the result will never be the same; that the reasons he gives for interference in what he has no concern hold good for every kind of interference with our neighbors when we disapprove their conduct. Is it not strange that the descendants of those Pilgrim Fathers who crossed the Atlantic to preserve the freedom of their opinion have always proved themselves intolerant of the spiritual liberty of others.

R. E. LEE TO MRS. LEE, *December 27, 1856.* JONES, *Life and Letters of Robert Edward Lee, Soldier and Man, pp. 82-83.*

Secession Is Nothing But Revolution

Throughout his military career Lee managed to keep relatively free of politics, but in the turmoil which followed Republican victory and the election of Lincoln in November, 1860, direct questions were put to him concerning his stand and he had to make clear-cut answers. When asked whether a man's first allegiance was due his state or the Nation, Lee replied that he had been taught to believe and did believe that his first obligations were due Virginia.

This is what Lee wrote to his son Custis on January 23, 1861. At that time the states of South Carolina, Mississippi, Florida, Alabama, and Georgia had seceded and had seized the Federal fortications within their borders, and the South Carolina troops at Charleston had actually fired on a United States transport, "Star of the West," which had been sent with reinforcements for Fort Sumter.

he South, in my opinion, has been aggrieved by the acts of the North, as you say. I feel the aggression, and am willing to take every proper step for redress. It is the principle I contend for, not individual or private benefit. As an American citizen, I take great pride in my country, her prosperity and institutions, and would defend any State if her rights were invaded. But I can anticipate no greater calamity for the country than a dissolution of the Union. It would be an accumulation of all the evils we complain of, and I am willing to sacrifice everything but honor for its preservation. I hope, therefore, that all constitutional means will be exhausted before there is a resort to force. Secession is nothing but revolution. . . .

JONES, *Life and Letters of R. E. Lee, pp. 120-121.*

With his world falling apart and the men around him, even in his own command, choosing sides, Lee wrote Jan. 22, 1861, from his distant post in Texas to his favorite cousin, Martha Custis Williams, a letter in which he revealed the anguish in his heart.

God alone can save us from our folly, selfishness & shortsightedness. The last accounts seem to show that we have barely escaped anarchy to be plunged into civil war. What will be the result I cannot conjecture. I only see that a federal calamity is upon us, & fear that the country will have to pass through for its sins a fiery ordeal. I am unable to realize that our people will destroy a government inaugurated by the blood & wisdom of our patriot fathers, that has given us peace & prosperity at home, power & security abroad, & under which we have acquired a colossal strength unequalled in the history of mankind. I wish to live under no other government, & there is no sacrifice I am not ready to make for the preservation of the Union save that of honour. If a disruption takes place, I shall go back in sorrow to my people & share the misery of my native state, & save in her defence there will be one soldier less in the world than now. I wish for no other flag than the "Star Spangled Banner," & no other air than "Hail Columbia." I still hope the wisdom & patriotism of the nation will yet save it.

I am so remote from the scene of events & receive such excited & exaggerated accounts of the opinions & acts of our statesmen, that I am at a loss what to think. I believe that the South justly complains of the aggressions of the North, & I have believed that the North would cheerfully redress the grievances complained of. I see no cause of disunion, strife & civil war & I pray it may be averted.

My own troubles, anxieties & sorrows sink into insignificance when I contemplate the sufferings present & prospective of the nation. Yet I am very desirous to be near those who claim my protection, & who may need my assistance. Nothing prevents my endeavoring to do so, but the necessity of my presence with the Regiment. There is no other field officer with it, & the presence of the officers may do much to quiet the apprehensions of the men, who are impatient under the present prospect of affairs, & absence of pay. We must endeavour to do our whole duty however far we know we fall short of it.

"To Markie." The Letters of Robert E. Lee to Martha Custis Williams, pp. 58-59.

Has All Love for Their Country Died at the South?

As the blackest year in American history wore on, the events which so disturbed Robert E. Lee, were also most distressing to his wife. Mary Custis Lee, whose father was the adopted son of George Washington, had little sympathy for the secessionists. On February 9, 1861, she wrote to her friend Eliza Mackay Stiles in Savannah, Georgia, to enquire whether she "could approve of all these riotous proceedings."

as all love for and pride in their country died at the South? That they are willing to tear her to pieces and *some* even to exult to see her glorious flag trailing in the dust. It should rather have driven tears from their eyes. We have lived and fought and prospered under this flag for so many years and tho' the South has suffered much from the *meddling* of Northern fanatics, yet do they expect to fare better now? Are there no rights and privileges but those of negro slavery? . . . I would lay down my life, could I save our "Union." What is the use of a Government combined as ours is of so many parts, the *union* of which forms its strength and power, if any *one part* has the right, for any wrong, real or imaginary, of withdrawing its aid and throwing the whole into confusion, as Carolina, who refuses all overtures for peace and imagines the world will admire her independence, whereas they laugh at her folly, which is perfectly suicidal. You know my feelings are all linked with the South and you will bear with me in the expression of my opinion, but while there are many of the Northern politicians who deserve no better fate than to be hung as high as Haman, believe me that those who have been *foremost* in this Revolution will deserve to meet with the reprobation of the World, either North or South, for having destroyed the most glorious Confederacy that ever existed. You have lived abroad. You have known many excellent people at the North and all your sympathies and feelings cannot be confined to your *state* to the exclusion of your *Country*. The Almighty may intend to punish us for our National Pride. I pray now that He will preserve us from Civil War. We can never boast again as a nation unless all could be restored.

Believe me, my dear friend, whatever may happen, you and yours will be always dear to my heart and at least our love and association will be unbroken. I only wish the other Southern States had left Carolina *alone* and the government had left her alone and she would soon have been tired of her *sovereignty*. She has been restless and anxious to show her independence for many years and it would have been well for her to try the experiment alone.

MRS. LEE TO MRS. WILLIAM HENRY STILES, *February 9, 1861.*
MS. Robert E. Lee Memorial Foundation, Inc., Stratford Hall Plantation, Virginia.

Save in Defense of My Native State

In February, 1861, after the secession of Texas, my father was ordered to report to General Scott, the Commander-in-Chief of the United States Army. He immediately relinquished the command of his regiment, and departed from Fort Mason, Texas, for Washington. He reached Arlington March 1st. April 17th, Virginia seceded. On the 18th Colonel Lee had a long interview with General Scott. On April 20th he tendered his resignation of his commission in the United States Army. The same day he wrote to General Scott the following letter:

"Arlington, Virginia, April 20, 1861.
"*General:* Since my interview with you on the 18th inst. I have felt that I ought no longer to retain my commission in the Army I therefore tender my resignation, which I request you will recommend for acceptance. It would have been presented at once but for the struggle it has cost me to separate myself from a service to which I have devoted the best years of my life, and all the ability I possessed.

"During the whole of that time—more than a quarter of a century—I have experienced nothing but kindness from my superiors and a most cordial friendship from my comrades. To no one, General, have I been as much indebted as to yourself for uniform kindness and consideration, and it has always been my ardent desire to merit your approbation. I shall carry to the grave the most grateful recollections of your kind consideration, and your name and fame shall always be dear to me.

"Save in the defense of my native State, I never desire again to draw my sword.

"Be pleased to accept my most earnest wishes for the continuance of your happiness and prosperity, and believe me most truly yours."

R. E. Lee."

R. E. Lee [Jr.], *Recollections and Letters, pp. 24-25.*

After his return to Virginia, Lee watched the events which followed so rapidly with great interest and fully sympathized with his native Virginia in the efforts she made to preserve the Union by refusing to join the seceding States. To the end he hoped that the Union might continue, and on March 28, he did not hesitate to accept a promotion to full colonel, in command of the 1st Cavalry of the United States. This commission was signed by Abraham Lincoln.

Robert E. Lee Is the Greatest Soldier Now Living

Virginia seceded April 17, 1861, but this news did not reach Washington until April 18, and Lee read it first in an Alexandria newspaper on April 19. That night he searched his soul as he paced his bedroom floor frequently kneeling to ask God's guidance. By the decision he was bound to make, he was destined to assume the responsibility for leading the Southern people in a tragic civil war which he neither desired nor thought was necessary. By following the fortunes of his native Virginia he was to make greater sacrifices than any man, North or South.

On April 18, by authority of President Lincoln, the command of the United States Army was offered to Robert E. Lee.

Hon. Simon Cameron of Pennsylvania, Mr. Lincoln's first Secretary of War, in an interview with a correspondent of the *New York Herald,* on the occasion of his 88th birthday, said:

". . . It is true that Gen. Robert E. Lee was tendered the command of the Union Army. It was the wish of Mr. Lincoln's Administration that as many as possible of the Southern officers then in the Regular Army should remain true to the nation which had educated them. Robert E. Lee and Joseph E. Johnston were the leading Southern soldiers. Johnston was Quartermaster-General and Lee a colonel of cavalry.

"In the moves and counter moves in the game of war and peace then going on, Francis P. Blair, Sr., was a prominent figure. The tender of command of our forces was made to General Lee through him. Mr. Blair came to me expressing the opinion that General Lee could be held to our cause by the offer of the chief command of our forces. I authorized Mr. Blair to make the offer. I then dismissed the matter from my mind as nearly as I could such an important subject, for I supposed from what Mr. Blair had said, that General Lee would certainly accept. I labored under this impression up to the time that his resignation was received. Whether General Lee ever seriously considered the matter I do not personally know. From what Senator Blair said to me I never had any doubt at the time but that he did. My surprise was great when the resignation was received and General Lee went South."

At daylight on April 12 the bombardment of Fort Sumter began. On the 14th Sumter surrendered without the loss of a single life on either side, and the next day, to a nation that had gone mad, Lincoln issued his proclamation calling for 75,000 volunteers "to suppress combinations" and "to cause the laws to be duly executed."

The war had begun and there could be but little doubt on which side the sword of Robert Lee would be drawn. He was the son of "Light Horse Harry," and a Virginian of the Virginians. He remembered that his father had said, in a debate on the famous resolutions of 1798-99, drawn by Mr. Madison, "Virginia is my country; her will I obey, however lamentable the fate to which it may subject me. . . ."

. . . Robert Edward Lee regarded his allegiance to the sovereign State of Virginia as paramount to all other.

. . . He regarded any attempt to "pin the States in the Union with the bayonet" as a violation of the fundamental principles for which the fathers fought in 1776. . . .

In a public address delivered in Baltimore soon after the death of General Lee, Hon. Reverdy Johnson [Senator from Maryland] said: "I was with General Scott in April, 1861, when he received the resignation of General Lee, and witnessed the pain it caused him. It was a sad blow to the success of that war, in which his own sword had as yet been unsheathed. Much as General Scott regretted it, he never failed to say that he was convinced that Lee had taken that step from an imperative sense of duty. General Scott was consoled in a great measure by the reflection that he would have as his opponent a soldier worthy of every man's esteem, and one who would conduct the war upon the strictest rules of civilized warfare. There would be no outrages committed on private persons or property which he could prevent.

To a prominent banker of New York, who was very intimate with General Scott, the general said a short time before the war: " I tell you, sir, that Robert E. Lee is the greatest soldier now living, and if he ever gets the opportunity, he will prove himself the greatest captain in history."

JONES, *Life and Letters of Robert E. Lee, Soldier and Man, pp. 125-129.*

Two days after he resigned his commission in the United States Army, Lee went to Richmond at the invitation of the Governor and accepted command of the forces of the Commonwealth of Virginia with the rank of major general.

The Lee home—"Arlington House"—*from an original water color by Benson J. Lossing, 1853. In the Custis-Lee Mansion Museum, the Robert E. Lee Memorial, Arlington, Virginia, Courtesy, National Park Service.*

III. MAKE YOUR PLANS FOR SEVERAL YEARS OF WAR

Meanwhile, Mrs. Lee stubbornly remained at Arlington, hoping that somehow the impending calamity might be averted. On April 26 the General wrote from Richmond to his wife:

I am very anxious about you. You have to move and make arrangements to go to some point of safety, which you must select. The Mount Vernon plate and pictures ought to be secured. . . . War is inevitable, and there is no telling when it will burst around you. Virginia, yesterday, I understand, joined the Confederate States. What policy they may adopt I cannot conjecture. . . .

Lee wrote his wife again on April 30:

On going to my room last night I found my trunk and sword there, and opening them this morning discovered the package of letters and was very glad to learn you were all well and as yet peaceful. I fear the latter state will not continue long. . . . I think therefore you had better prepare all things for removal, that is, the plate, pictures, etc., and be prepared at any moment. Where to go is the difficulty. When the war commences no place will be exempt, in my opinion, and indeed all the avenues into the State will be the scenes of military operations.

R. E. Lee [Jr.], *Recollections and Letters, p. 29.*

In the same letter Lee wrote the following:

I wrote to Robert [his son] that I could not consent to take boys from their schools and young men from their colleges and put them in the ranks at the beginning of the war when they are not needed. The war may last ten years. Where are our ranks to be filled from then?

Fitzhugh Lee, *General Lee, p. 93.*

And Mrs. Lee, from Arlington, May 5, sent the following note to General Scott in Washington:

"My Dear General: Hearing that you desire to see the account of my husband's reception in Richmond, I have sent it to you. No honors can reconcile us to this fratricidal war which we would have laid down our lives freely to avert. Whatever may happen, I feel that I may expect from your kindness all the protection you can in honor afford. Nothing can ever make me forget your kind appreciation of Mr. Lee. If you knew all you would not think so hardly of me. Were it not that I would not add one feather to his load of care, nothing would induce me to abandon my home. Oh, that you could command peace to our distracted country! Yours in sadness and sorrow,

M. C. Lee."

Occasionally this wife and mother's heart would beat with happiness at the stories of successful compromise between the sections and then sink in despair at the continued prospects of war.

From Richmond, May 13, 1861, her husband wrote her:

"Do not put faith in rumors of adjustment. I see no prospect for it. It can not be while passions on both sides are so infuriated. Make your plans for several years of war. If Virginia is invaded, which appears to be designed, the main routes through the country will, in all probability, be infested and passage interrupted. I agree with you in thinking that the inflammatory articles in the papers do us much harm. I object particularly to those in the Southern papers, as I wish them to take a firm, dignified course, free from bravado and boasting. The times are indeed calamitous. The brightness of God's countenance seems turned from us, and its mercy stopped in its blissful current. It may not always be so dark, and he may in time pardon our sins and take us under his protection. . . ."

FITZHUGH LEE, *General Lee, pp. 93-94.*

About May 14, Mary Custis Lee reluctantly left Arlington forever.

Invasion of Virginia

Events moved swiftly in the spring and early summer of 1861. Virginia joined the Confederate States. The capital of the new southern confederacy was moved to Richmond. And Lee, now a brigadier general in the Confederate Army, became military adviser to President Jefferson Davis with responsibility for all Confederate forces in the State of Virginia.

On the 24th of May the advance guard of the Federal army occupied the heights of Washington, with Arlington, the former home of General Lee, as headquarters, as well as all the country stretching down the Potomac eight miles below to Alexandria. Only a few persons understood the magnitude of the impending contest. The "Rebellion" many thought was to be crushed in ninety days, and most of the volunteer troops were enlisted by the North for that period.

One hundred and fifteen miles away, at Richmond, great activity prevailed also. The sagacity, skill, and experience of Lee were taxed to the uttermost equipping and sending to threatened points the troops rapidly arriving from the South. There was no regular army to serve as a nucleous, or navy, commissary, quartermaster's, or ordnance departments. Everything had to be provided. General [Josiah] Gorgas, the Chief of Ordnance of the Confederate States, reported that he found in all the arsenals of the Confederate States but fifteen thousand rifles and one hundred and twenty thousand inferior muskets. In addition there were a few old flint muskets at Richmond, and some Hall's rifles and carbines at Baton Rouge. There was no powder, except some which had been left over from the Mexican War and had been stored at Baton Rouge Arsenal and at Mount Vernon, Ala. There was but little artillery, and no cavalry, arms, or equipments. Raw recruits had to be drilled and disciplined, companies assigned to regiments, regiments to brigades, brigades to divisions. With the map of Virginia before him, Lee studied to make a successful defensive campaign. He knew that the object of the greatest importance to his enemy was the capture of Richmond, and the fall of that city early in the contest might terminate the war. His genius for grand tactics and strategy taught him at once that the most natural advance to Richmond from Washington would be along the Orange and Alexandria Railroad, as it was called then. It was the only railway running into the State at that time from Washington, and troops moving along its line could be so directed as not to uncover their capital, while prompt facilities could be obtained for transportation of supplies from the base established at Alexandria or Washington. Another route lay up the peninsula lying between the James and York Rivers, with Fort Monroe and its vicinity as a base for operations. Another way to enter the State was by crossing the upper Potomac at Harper's Ferry and Williamsport, and then on through the great valley of Virginia between the Blue Ridge and Shenandoah Mountains; and still another entrance might be effected through the mountain ranges of West Virginia, Norfolk, too, by the sea, had to be watched and protected. Troops, therefore, as fast as they arrived in Richmond and could be prepared for the campaign, were sent principally to these points. It was necessary that organized forces should be in such position as to check any forward movements by any of these routes. General Lee early had predicted the march of the Army of the Potomac, as the Washington army was called, and pointed out what would in all probability be the battlefield. He ordered the largest number of troops to Manassas Junction, that being the point of union of the railroad coming into Virginia from Washington with a branch road leading into the Valley of Virginia. It was a strategic point, because an army in position there would be able to resist the further progress of the opposing hosts, and could, if necessary, re-enforce the troops in the valley. Competent and experienced officers were at an early date placed in command of the important stations. For Manassas, General P. G. T. Beauregard was selected. This officer, having been the first employed in active operations, and having compelled the surrender of Fort Sumter, was the military hero of the hour. . . .

Irvin McDowell, the commander selected to lead the Federal army against its opponent at Manassas, was a native of Ohio, and graduated at the Military Academy at West Point in 1838.

FITZHUGH LEE, *General Lee, pp. 99-101, 106.*

The battle fought at Manassas on July 21 termnated in the defeat of McDowell's army, which was thrown back in confusion toward Washington. From Richmond, on July 27th, Lee wrote to his wife:

That indeed was a glorious victory and has lightened the pressure upon our front amazingly. Do not grieve for the brave dead. Sorrow for those they left behind—friends, relatives, and families. The former are at rest. The latter must suffer. The battle will be repeated there in greater force. I hope God will again smile on us and strengthen our hearts and arms. I wished to partake in the former struggle, and am mortified at my absence, but the President thought it more important I should be here. I could not have done as well as has been done, but I could have helped, and taken part in the struggle for my home and neighborhood. So the work is done I care not by whom it is done. I leave tomorrow for the Northwest Army. . . .

R. E. Lee [JR.], *Recollections and Letters, p. 37.*

Rain, Rain, Nothing But Rain

Lee's first campaign in the field ended in failure which might have been averted or diminished had he been less the gentleman and more the soldier. He was handicapped by an exaggerated sense of consideration for the feelings of subordinate officers. The highlights of this campaign are given by Colonel Walter H. Taylor, who, from the beginning to the end of the war, was a member of Lee's staff.

In the northwest the Confederate forces under Brigadier-General Robert S. Garnett . . . had suffered defeat, and the brave Garnett himself, while endeavoring to rally his troops at Carricksford, had received a mortal wound. Brigadier-General W. W. Loring had been assigned as his successor in the command of this department, and having collected the scattered remnants of Garnett's little army, together with such reenforcements as the Government had been able to send to his relief, had taken position at Valley Mountain. In the southwest Brigadier-Generals Floyd and Wise were operating under great disadvantages; each having an independent command, and neither being disposed to act a part subordinate to the other. It was impossible, under such circumstances, to secure harmonious action or any united and spirited effort to resist the enemy. There was an evident and imperative need in this quarter for the personal presence of some one who could both restore confidence to the troops and compel the respect and subordination of commanders. General Lee, of all men the most fit for this duty, was also the most available . . . immediately after the first battle of Manassas, General Lee was dispatched to the scene of operations in that department to reconcile the differences between Brigadier-Generals Floyd and Wise, and to aid Brigadier-General Loring in the reorganization and recruiting of the shattered forces of Garnett, so that, with the aid of the reenforcements sent, the army there collected might be put in such condition as to prevent any aggressive movement of the enemy, and, if circumstances justified it, to take the offensive. . . .

On arrival at Valley Mountain, Lee discovered that prompt action against the enemy was desirable, but Loring planned first to build up a supply depot in advance of action, and Lee, reluctant to assert his authority, deferred to Loring, and planned a later assault on Cheat Mountain, the Union stronghold on the crest of the Alleghanies. Lee never assumed personal command of the army, although it was understood that Loring was subject to his orders.

It is useless to attempt to recount all the difficulties this little army encountered in that most impracticable, inhospitable, and dismal country; only those who participated in that campaign can ever properly estimate the disadvantages under which commanders and troops operated. The season was a most unfavorable one: for weeks it rained daily and in torrents; the condition of the roads was frightful; they were barely passable. It was very seriously debated whether the army could be fed where it was, and it was feared that it would have to retire to some point nearer the railroad. Time and time again could be seen double teams of horses struggling with six or eight barrels of flour, and the axle of the wagon scraping and leveling the road-bed; in other words, the wagons were hub-deep in mud, and could only be moved step by step, and then with the greatest difficulty. At the same time, and doubtless as a result of the excessive rains, the troops were sorely afflicted with measles and a malignant type of fever, which prostrated hundreds of each command; and, being entirely destitute of proper food and other supplies indispensable to the successful treatment of disease, it is not to be wondered at that medical skill failed to arrest the terrible scourge.

Moreover, although some of our best and bravest men were from that section, there was great dissatisfaction among that portion of the people who had not responded to the

call of the State for troops. Spies lurked around every hill; our weakness, our embarrass-
ments, and our every movement, were promptly reported to the enemy. With some honorable exceptions, there was an utter absence of sympathy on the part of the inhabitants
who had remained at home, and, to all intents and purposes, we were in the enemy's
country. In the language of another who witnessed this deplorable hostility: "Northwest-
ern Virginia has brought grief and shame to the State and to the South by her woeful
defection; . . ."

TAYLOR, *Four Years with General Lee, pp. 15-18.*

*The hopelessness of the situation was reflected in a letter written September 3 by Lee to his
son, Custis:*

I have been able to do but little here. Still I hope I have been of some service. Things
are better organized. I feel stronger, we are stronger. The three routes leading east are
guarded. The men have more confidence, our people a feeling of security. The enemy has
been driven back, and made to haul in his horns, and to find he cannot have everything
his own way. This has been done without a battle, but by a steady advance of positions.
Now to drive him farther a battle must come off, and I am anxious to begin it. Circumstances beyond human control delay it, I know for good, but I hope the Great Ruler of
the Universe will continue to aid and prosper us, and crown at last our feeble efforts with
success. Rain, rain, rain, there has been nothing but rain. So it has appeared to my anxious
mind since I approached these mountains. It commenced before, but since has come down
with a will. The cold too has been greater than I could have conceived. In my winter
clothing and buttoned up in my overcoat, I have still been cold. This state of the weather
has aggravated the sickness that has attacked the whole army, measles and typhoid fever.
Some regiments have not over 250 for duty, some 300, 500, or about half, according to its
strength. This makes a terrible hole in our effectiveness. Do not mention this, I pray you.
It will be in the papers next. . . .

JONES, *Life and Letters of Robert Edward Lee, Soldier and Man, pp. 146-147.*

*The battle for Cheat Mountain, which Lee was very anxious to begin, was planned with ex-
treme care. Reconnaissance had revealed the character of the defenses and an unguarded flank
up the mountain. Success depended on surprise, the utmost secrecy, and coordination of all
movements. The most difficult assignment was given to Colonel Albert Rust, of the Third Arkansas Regiment. With his command he was to ascend the mountain, and having reached the
crest, he was to fire the signal for all units to attack. According to Colonel Taylor, this is
what happened:*

The several commands, being in every respect prepared for the anticipated battle,
moved forward at the time mentioned, and in the several directions indicated, in the order
of march and attack.

All progressed satisfactorily. Anderson reached and occupied the turnpike at its crossing on the third or rear top of Cheat Mountain. So unsuspecting was the enemy, and so
silently was Anderson's movement made, that his men captured an engineer-officer of
Rosencrans's staff, and others, quietly and confidently pursuing the road toward their rear.

General [Henry R.] Jackson had his command well in hand, prepared to engage the
enemy in front.

General Donelson's brigade rested the latter portion of the night not far from the
camps of his enemy on Tygart's Valley River.

Morning found everything just as the most confident could have hoped, with the exception that the night had been a very rainy, disagreeable one, and the men were conse-
quently quite uncomfortable; this, however, would soon be forgotten in the excitement of
battle and the promise of certain victory. All was ready, and Rust's attack was anxiously
awaited. General Jackson worried the enemy considerably by attacking his advanced
guard on the first top of the mountain, only awaiting the signal from Rust to press forward
earnestly with his entire command. Hours passed, and no signal was heard! What could

have happened? Enough time had elapsed to enable the troops to reach Centre-top, unless prevented by some unexpected impediment.

Would Rust *never* attack? Alas! He never did!

As was subsequently learned, upon an examination of the works of the enemy made after he had succeeded in reaching his proper position, he was surprised to find them far more formidable than he had supposed. Whether additional strength had been given them since his reconnaissance, or whether he was too easily satisfied and not sufficiently thorough in his observations when he made that reconnaissance, is not known. He decided that the works were too formidable to justify an assault, and no attack was made. Even had he discharged his guns and vigorously engaged the enemy, without attempting to carry the works by storm, it is not unreasonable to believe that the combined efforts of the other columns would have been attended with success.

TAYLOR, *Four Years with General Lee, pp. 27-28.*

Lee reported the failure of the battle to Governor Letcher. "But for the rain-storm," he concluded, "I have no doubt it would have succeeded . . . we must try again." But there was to be no second chance in this campaign. The rains continued to fall. There was no battle, and one morning in the early days of October, it was discovered that during the previous night Rosencrans had pulled back to a point nearer his base of supplies Lee was left with his shivering men facing the empty rain-swept mountains.

Neither the people nor the press of Virginia understood the difficulties of this campaign or the role played by Lee. They expected of him far more than he could accomplish and denounced him for not driving the Federal forces out of the State.

When Mrs. Lee wrote to her husband about the harsh criticism in the newspapers concerning his conduct of the campaign, he replied:

I am sorry, as you say, that the movements of the armies cannot keep pace with the expectations of the editors of papers. I know they can regulate matters satisfactorily to themselves on paper. I wish they could do so in the field. No one wishes them more success than I do and would be happy to see them have full swing. I hope something will be done to please them. . . .

R. E. LEE [JR.], *Recollections and Letters, p. 51.*

Worse Than Western Virginia

The defenseless condition of the States south of Virginia bordering on the Atlantic coast was an object of solicitude to the Confederate War Department. Important seaports and the sections adjoining them were at the mercy of combined Federal fleets and armies. Their proper defense was most difficult, the means most inadequate. It was a good field for a capable engineer. Lee was available, and the emergency demanded his services. Reluctantly he was ordered from Richmond, cheerfully he obeyed, and on November 6th proceeded to South Carolina, where he at once commenced to erect a line of defense along the Atlantic coasts of that State, Georgia, and Florida.

His four months' labors in this department brought prominently into view his skill. Exposed points were no longer in danger. Well-conceived defensive works rose rapidly. Public confidence in that department was permanently restored, and with it came to Lee a new accession of popularity and esteem. His headquarters was wisely established at Coosawhatchie on the railroad, a point midway between Charleston, S. C., and Savannah, Ga., and from which he could give close supervision to the defenses of these important cities. . . .

FITZHUGH LEE, *General Lee, p. 128.*

Lee arrived at his new post of November 7, 1861. On this same day combined army and naval forces struck at Port Royal Sound on the coast of South Carolina. After a short but fierce bombardment, the Navy knocked out the two forts at the entrance to the sound, and the Army landed unopposed on Hilton Head Island. The defenders of this outpost beat a hasty retreat to the mainland, and the city of Savannah was thrown into panic.

It was imperative that Lee move swiftly. Innumerable deep water inlets invited landings almost anywhere on the Georgia and South Carolina coasts, and invasion of the mainland could follow. Within two days of his arrival, Lee ordered the withdrawal of troops from the exposed islands and began to strengthen the mainland fortifications.

The following excerpts from Lee's letters to his wife and daughters provide an intimate view of what he was doing and what he was thinking during this strenuous period.

To his daughter, Mildred:

Charleston, S. C., November 15, 1861.

I was unable to see your poor mother when in Richmond. Before I could get down I was sent off here. Another forlorn hope expedition. Worse than Western Virginia. . . .

To his daughter, Annie:

Coosawhatchie, S. C., December 8, 1861.

I am trying to get a force to make headway on our defenses, but it comes in very slow. The people do not seem to realize that there is a war.

To Mrs. Lee.

Coosawhatchie, S. C., Christmas Day, 1861.

You must not build your hopes on peace on account of the United States going into a war with England. She will be very loath to do that, notwithstanding the bluster of the Northern papers. Her rulers are not entirely mad. . . . We must make up our minds to fight our battles and win our independence alone. No one will help us. We require no extraneous aid, if true to ourselves. But we must be patient. It is not a light achievement and cannot be accomplished at once. . . .

Confederates abandon *Fort Walker at Hilton Head, South Carolina, November 7, 1861. From a wartime sketch by W. T. Crane in Frank Leslie's Illustrated Newspaper, December 7, 1861.*

35

To Mrs. Lee.

Savannah, February 8, 1862.

I wrote to you, dear Mary, the day I left Coosawhatchie for this place. I have been here ever since, endeavouring to push forward the work for the defense of the city, which has lagged terribly and which ought to have been finished. But it is difficult to arouse ourselves from ease and comfort to labour and self-denial.

Guns are scarce, as well as ammunition, and I shall have to break up batteries on the coast to provide, I fear, for this city. Our enemies are endeavouring to work their way through the creeks that traverse the impassable and soft marshes stretching along the interior of the coast and communicating with the sounds and sea, through which the Savannah flows, and thus avoid the entrance of the river commanded by Fort Pulaski. Their boats require only seven feet of water to float them, and the tide rises seven feet, so that at high water they can work their way and rest on the mud at low. They also are provided with dredges and appliances for removing obstructions through the creeks in question, which cannot be guarded by batteries. I hope, however, we shall be able to stop them, and I daily pray to the Giver of all victories to enable us to do so. . . . I hope God will at last crown our efforts with success. But the contest must be long and severe, and the whole country has to go through much suffering. . . .

To his daughter, Annie:

Savannah, March 2, 1862.

My Precious Annie: It has been a long time since I have written to you, but you have been constantly in my thoughts. I think of you all, separately and collectively, in the busy hours of the day and the silent hours of the night, and the recollection of each and every one whiles away the long night, in which my anxious thoughts drive away sleep. But I always feel that you and Agnes at those times are sound asleep, and that it is immaterial to either where the blockaders are or what their progress is in the river. I hope you are all well, and as happy as you can be in these perilous times to our country. They look dark at present, and it is plain we have not suffered enough, laboured enough, repented enough, to deserve success. But they will brighten after awhile, and I trust that a merciful God will arouse us to a sense of our danger, bless our honest efforts, and drive back our enemies to their homes. Our people have not been earnest enough, have thought too much of themselves and their ease, and instead of turning out to a man, have been content to nurse themselves and their dimes, and leave the protection of themselves and families to others. To satisfy their consciences, they have been clamourous in criticising what others have done, and endeavoured to prove that they ought to do nothing. This is not the way to accomplish our independence. I have been doing all I can with our small means and slow workmen to defend the cities and coast here. Against ordinary numbers we are pretty strong, but against the hosts our enemies seem able to bring everywhere there is no calculating. But if our men will stand to their work, we shall give them trouble and damage them yet. They have worked their way across the marshes, with their dredges, under cover of their gunboats, to the Savannah River, above Fort Pulaski. I presume they will endeavour to reduce the fort and thus open a way for their vessels up the river. But we have an interior line they must force before reaching the city. It is on this line we are working, slowly to my anxious mind, but as fast as I can drive them. . . . Good-bye, my dear child. May God bless you and our poor country.

Your devoted father,
R. E. Lee.

R. E. LEE [JR.], *Recollections and Letters, pp. 54-66.*

On the day this letter was written, Lee received a telegram from Jefferson Davis recalling him to Richmond.

He Never Gets Any Credit
For What He Has Done

Lee was already back in Richmond when his wife began the following letter to Mrs. William Henry Stiles in Savannah.

White House (Va.), March 8th 1862.

I have been intending to write to you for some time, my dear friend, but did not know exactly where you were, but tonight when a letter from Mr. Lee to Annie informed me that you were in Savannah and had taken my husband and his wardrobe in charge, I could not delay a moment to express my satisfaction. I have heard of nothing that has given me so much pleasure since our last success. I know now that he is in good hands and will be well taken care of. If I could only be with you all. . . . Poor Virginia is pressed on every side.

11th. I had written this far when I saw my husband's arrival announced in the paper and last Sunday I had the satisfaction of seeing him for one day after a separation of nearly a year. He looks well in spite of his cares and I see by the papers that he is put in charge of the armies of the Confederacy. Now they have got into trouble they send for him to help them out, and yet he never gets any credit for what he has done. . . . He never complains or seems to desire anything more than to perform his duty, but I may be excused for wishing him to reap the reward of his labors.

Affectionately yours,
M. C. Lee

MRS. LEE TO MRS. WILLIAM HENRY STILES, *March 8, 1862*
MS. Robert E. Lee Memorial Foundation, Inc., Stratford Hall Plantation, Virginia.

The papers in which Mrs. Lee had read the above notice were premature in their announcements, for Jefferson Davis, jealous of his constitutional rights as commander-in-chief, vetoed the bill by which Congress authorized him to nominate a commanding general. Simultaneously, he assigned General Lee "to duty at the seat of government" charged "under the direction of the President with the conduct of military operations in the armies of the Confederacy."

Douglas Southall Freeman, in his great biography of Lee, characterizes this appointment as "an impossible assignment." "In his whole career," says Freeman, "there was not a period of more thankless service, but there were few, if any, during which he contributed more to sustain the Confederate cause."

In a letter to his wife, written from Richmond, March 14, 1862, Lee explains:

I have been placed on duty here to conduct operations under the direction of the President. It will give me great pleasure to do anything I can to relieve him and serve the country, but I do not see either advantage or pleasure in my duties. But I will not complain, but will do my best. . . .

R. E. LEE [JR.], Recollections and Letters, pp. 66-67.

The King of Spades

In April, 1862 McClellan brought the Army of the Potomac to Fort Monroe, with the intention of marching up the peninsula between the York and James rivers to Richmond. Magruder, who was guarding this approach to the Confederate capital, had prepared a strong defense line across the peninsula at Yorktown. When McClellan began to probe this line, Confederate General Joseph E. Johnston moved the greater part of his forces from the Rappahannock to Yorktown and assumed command. Meanwhile "Stonewall" Jackson was conducting a campaign in the Valley of Virginia which, serving as a threat against Washington, pinned down an army of 40,000 under McDowell, which President Lincoln had insisted should be held in reserve for the defense of the Federal Capital.

The Yorktown line did not please Johnston as it could be turned on both flanks by gunboats passing up the York and James rivers. He proposed to give battle at a point near Richmond. As this would necessitate the evacuation of Norfolk, and the destruction of the Ironclad Merrimack, the proposal was turned down by President Davis. Nevertheless, on May 4, Johnston withdrew from Yorktown and began a slow retreat up the peninsula. McClellan's forces numbered better than 100,000. Johnston had about 53,000.

On May 31, at Seven Pines, Johnston took the offensive and attempted to check the Federal Juggernaut. In the course of a confused battle, which brought no particular advantage to either side, Johnston was badly wounded. Present as observers were both President Davis and General Lee, and Davis on the battlefield within 5 miles of the capital determined to place Lee in command of the defense of Richmond.

Very early the next morning, General Lee received the following note:

Johnston *abandons Mechanicsville, May 24, 1862.*

Richmond, Va., June 1, 1862.

General R. E. Lee.

Sir: The unfortunate casualty which has deprived the army in front of Richmond of its immediate commander, General Johnston, renders it necessary to interfere temporarily with the duties to which you were assigned in connection with the general service, but only so far as to make you available for command in the field of a particular army. You will assume command of the army in Eastern Virginia and in North Carolina, and give such orders as may be needed and proper.

Very respectfully,
JEFFERSON DAVIS.

On the receipt of this note, Lee published:
Special Orders No. 22

Headquarters, Richmond, Va., June 1, 1862.

I. In pursuance of the orders of the President, General R. E. Lee assumes command of the armies of Eastern Virginia and North Carolina.

The unfortunate casualty that has deprived the army in front of Richmond of the valuable services of its able general is not more deeply deplored by any member of his command than by its present commander. He hopes his absence will be but temporary, and while he will endeavor to the best of his ability to perform his duties, he feels he will be totally inadequate to the task unless he shall receive the cordial support of every officer and man.

The presence of the enemy in front of the capital, the great interests involved, and the existence of all that is dear to us appeal in terms too strong to be unheard, and he feels assured that every man has resolved to maintain the ancient fame of the Army of Northern Virginia and the reputation of its general and to conquer or die in the approaching contest.

II. Commanders of divisions and brigades will take every precaution and use every means in their power to have their commands in readiness at all times for immediate action. They will be careful to preserve their men as much as possible, that they may be fresh when called upon for active service. All surplus baggage, broken-down wagons, horses, and mules, and everything that may embarrass the prompt and speedy movement of the army will be turned into depot. Only sufficient transportation will be retained for carrying the necessary cooking utensils and such tents or tent-flies as are indispensable to the comfort and protection of the troops.

By order of General Lee:

W. H. TAYLOR,
Assistant Adjutant-General

Official Records of the Union and Confederate Armies,
Series I, Vol. 11, Part 3, pp. 568-569.

The troops politely cheered when this order was read to them, but there was no enthusiasm. To date, Lee had commanded no troops in the field; he had won no battles; but through the prodigious amount of earthworks he had caused to be constructed, he had earned the title, "The King of Spades."

He Will Take More Desperate Chances Than Any Other General

There was considerable trepidation among Johnston's lieutenants when Lee assumed command of the army. Would he be bold enough to assure success? Aside from Davis about the only man of station who seemed to realize what Lee might accomplish in the field, was Johnston himself. A few days after the Battle of Seven Pines, when told by a friend that his wounding was a calamity to the South, Johnston answered:

o sir. The shot that struck me down is the very best that has been fired for the Southern Confederacy yet. For I possess in no degree the confidence of our government, and now they have in my place one who does possess it, and who can accomplish what I never could have done,—the concentration of our armies for the defence of the capital of the Confederacy.

Johnston quoted in: DABNEY H. MAURY, Recollections of a Virginian, p. 151.

Johnston was completely sincere in his estimate of Lee. Said he at a much later date:

No one among men but his own brothers had better opportunity to know General Lee than I. We entered the Military Academy together as classmates, and formed then a friendship never impaired. It was formed very soon after we met, from the fact that my father served under his in the celebrated Lee's Legion. We had the same intimate associates, who thought, as I did, that no other youth or man so united the qualities that win warm friendship and command high respect. For he was full of sympathy and kindness, genial and fond of gay conversation, and even of fun, that made him the most agreeable of companions, while his correctness of demeanor and language and attention to all duties, personal and official, and a dignity as much a part of himself as the elegance of his person, gave him a superiority that every one acknowledged in his heart. He was the only one of all the men I have known who could laugh at the faults and follies of his friends in such a manner as to make them ashamed without touching their affection for him, and to confirm their respect and sense of his superiority.

LONG, Memoirs of Robert E. Lee, p. 71.

In a very short time, Lee won over most of his critics through his faultless manner, his energy, and his willingness to assume the responsibility of leadership. He inspired confidence in those who got to know him well. When Lee had been in command about two weeks, for instance, Major E. P. Alexander was riding with Colonel Joseph Ives, who had been Lee's engineer in South Carolina and was now on President Davis's staff. They were talking of Lee.

"Ives," said Alexander, "tell me this. We are here fortifying our lines, but apparently leaving the enemy all the time he needs to accumulate his superior forces, and then to move on us in the way he thinks best. Has Gen. Lee the *audacity* that is going to be required for our inferior force to meet the enemy's superior force,—to take the aggressive, and to run risks and stand chances?"

Ives's reply was so impressive, both in manner and matter, that it has always been remembered as vividly as if to-day. He reined up his horse, stopped in the road, and, turning to me, said: "Alexander, if there is one man in either army, Confederate or Federal, head and shoulders above every other in *audacity*, it is Gen. Lee! His name might be Audacity. He will take more desperate chances and take them quicker than any other general in this country, North or South; and you will live to see it, too."

E. P. ALEXANDER, Military Memoirs of a Confederate, pp. 110-111.

What Genius! What Audacity in Lee!

t last, one year after the commencement of the war, Robert E. Lee was in active command of a large army in the field. His task was difficult, his responsibility great. The opposing hosts were thundering at the city's gates. Inch by inch they had crept so close that spectators on the housetops could see their fire-fringed lines and hear the angry roar of their cannon. Upon his shoulders rested the safety of his capital. With quiet dignity he assumed his duties. . . .

In Lee, as with McClellan, the military engineer was combined with the army commander. Earthworks were rapidly constructed. The topographical features of the country were scientifically made available; and ere many days had passed the Southern troops were everywhere behind strong intrenchments, while between them and the city was a line of more permanent works, which had been constructed some time before as a precautionary measure, and behind which the troops could be rallied if the first lines were successfully assailed. Almost every day now a soldierly looking man, clad in a neat but simple gray uniform, conspicuous by the absence of the wreath, gold braids and stars usually found on the uniforms of general officers, sitting his horse like a dragoon, might be seen riding along the lines. No long column of staff or couriers followed him, no display, no ostentation, none of the pomp of war. . . .

FITZHUGH LEE, *General Lee, pp. 150-152.*

J. B. Jones, clerk in the Confederate War Department at Richmond, made the following notations in his diary in the summer of 1862:

June 13th—Gen. Lee is satisfied with the present posture of affairs—and McClellan has no idea of attacking us now. . . .

June 15th—What a change! No one now dreams of the loss of the capital.

June 18th—Lee is quietly preparing to attack McClellan. The President, who was on the battle-field is very cheerful.

Lee was indeed preparing to attack and his secret plan were already rapidly advancing. The first step was to procure exact information concerning McClellan's position and line of communications. To learn these facts, he sent Brigadier-General J. E. B. Stuart on a cavalry raid to the rear of McClellan's right. On the evening of June 12 Stuart set off joyously at the head of 1,200 hand picked men, headed first in the direction of the Valley as if to reinforce Jackson, then turned eastward and in little more than 48 hours rode completely around McClellan's army of 115,000 men in line of battle without the loss of a man. This adventure set the telegraph wires crackling with the news to the cities and towns of both North and South.

Richmond, June 15.—Brigadier Gen. Stewart [Stuart] has made a circuit through the enemy's line from Richmond via Hanover Court House and Old Church, Tunstall's, to James River and back to the city, where he arrived this morning. He captured one hundred and seventy-five prisoners, three hundred horses and mules, and destroyed three large transports on the Pamunkey River, loaded with commissary stores.

Savannah Morning News, June 16, 1862, p. 1, c. 1.

With the information he desired, Lee was now ready to take the offensive and on the evening of June 23 he held a council of war with his Lieutenants, "Stonewall" Jackson, D. H. Hill, A. P. Hill, and Longstreet. Following the conference the battle order was prepared.

Wrote the Rebel War Clerk:

June 24th.—Gen. Lee's plan works like a charm! Although I have daily orders from Mr. Randolph [Secretary of War] to send persons beyond our lines, yet the precautions of Lee most effectually prevent any spies from knowing anything about his army. Even the Adjutant-General, S. Cooper, don't know how many regiments are ordered into Virginia, or where they are stationed. Officers returning from furlough, cannot ascertain in the Adjutant-General's office where their regiments are! They are referred to me for passports to Gen. Lee's headquarters. . . . This is the harbinger of success, and I predict a career of glory for Lee, and for our country! There are some vague rumors about the approach of Stonewall Jackson's army; but no one knows anything about it, and but few believe it. Recent Northern papers say he is approaching Winchester, and I see they are intrenching in the valley to guard against his terrible blows. This is capital! . . .

It had been Lee's design to confuse the enemy as much as possible. He reinforced Jackson in the valley with the result that:

Mr. Lincoln telegraphed McClellan on June 20th that Jackson is being heavily reinforced from Richmond, and that he did not think he could send him more troops. Two days previous McClellan had informed Lincoln that some ten thousand troops from Lee's army had been sent to Jackson, to which the Union President replied that if the report were true, it would be as good as a re-enforcement to him of equal force, and that he would be glad to be informed what day he would attack Richmond. While these telegrams were being exchanged Jackson was rapidly moving to the support of Lee. The main portion of his army left the Valley on June 18th, marching by Charlottesville and Gordonsville, which latter place was reached on the 21st. . . .

The night of the 25th his command was encamped in the vicinity of Ashland, on the Richmond and Fredericksburg Railroad, some sixteen miles from Richmond. Early on the morning of the 26th he moved easterly, crossing the Central Railroad below Hanover Court House about ten o'clock, and, taking the Mechanicsville road, camped for the night south of the Totopatomoy Creek at a place called Hundley's Corner, some seven or eight miles northeast of Mechanicsville. . . .

Fitzhugh Lee, *General Lee, pp. 157-158.*

On June 26th the Rebel War Clerk wrote in his diary: "This is the day of the battle." And after enjoying his noon-time dinner, he went to a hilltop with friends to listen. Soon there was a fusilade of shots on the far left. A. P. Hill had begun the fight. "McClellan," he wrote; "must be thunderstruck at this unexpected opening of a decisive battle. . . ."

Franklin's Corps *falling back from Gaines' Mill, June 29, 1862. With Lee now in command at Richmond, the Federal tide had turned.*

As the shades of evening fall, the fire seems to increase in rapidity, and a gentle breeze rising as the stars come out, billows of smoke are wafted from the battle-field. And now, occasionally, we can distinctly see the bursting of shells in the air, aimed too high by the enemy, and exploding far this side of our line of battle.

Darkness is upon us, save the glimmer of the stars, as the sulphurous clouds sink into the humid valleys. But the flashes of the guns are visible on the horizon, followed by the deep intonations of the mighty engines of destruction, echoing and reverberating from hill to hill, and through the vast valley of the James in the rear.

Hundreds of men, women, and children were attracted to the heights around the city to behold the spectacle. From the Capitol and from the President's mansion, the vivid flashes of artillery could be seen; but no one doubted the result. It is only silence and inaction we dread. The firing ceased at nine o'clock P. M. The President was on the field, but did not interfere with Lee.

June 27th.—At the first dawn of day, the battle recommenced, farther round to the east. This was enough. The enemy had drawn in his right wing. And courier after courier announced the taking of his batteries by our brave defenders! But the battle rages loud and long, and the troops of Jackson's corps, like the march of Fate, still upon McClellan's right flank and rear. Jackson's horse, and the gallant Stuart, with his irresistable cavalry, have cut the enemy's communications with their base on the Pamunky. It is said they are burning their stores!

What genius! What audacity in Lee! He has absolutely taken the greater portion of his army to the north side of the Chickahominy, leaving McClellan's center and left wing on the south side, with apparently easy access to the city. This is (to the invaders) impenetrable strategy. The enemy believes Lee's main forces are *here*, and will never think of advancing. We have so completely closed the avenues of intelligence that the enemy has not been able to get the slightest intimation of our strength or the dispositions of our forces.

The Rebel War Clerk was over optimistic in his description of the effectiveness of Lee's effort effort to conceal his movements. A Confederate deserter on June 24 disclosed to McClellan that Jackson was approaching, and Jackson's progress was thereby so slowed that he did not arrive on the battlefield until near the close of the second day. Then with guns at trail, Hood's Texans passed through the tired ranks of Hill, and on the double advanced on the Federal lines scarcely firing a shot. Hundreds fell, but the onward rush never faltered. Under the sound of the shrill rebel yell, the division swept onward. The Federals panicked, threw away their guns and ran. A gap had been made, and now the whole Confederate line moved forward.

Lee's strategy had been predicated on the assumption that Richmond could not be successfully defended in a formal siege. It was necessary, then, for him to assume the offensive. The Federal positions were too strong for direct assault. Therefore, there must be a turning movement. Fortunately, for Lee, McClellan consistently overestimated the Confederate strength. In seven days of fighting, which gave to history the battle names of Mechanicsville, Gaines's Mill, Savage's Station, Frayser's Farm, and Malvern Hill, Lee cut McClellan's communications with the Pamunkey River and forced him to a new base on the James. Federal losses amounted to approximately 16,000 men, killed, wounded, and missing, and the Confederates gained 52 Federal guns and 31,000 small arms, but the Confederate losses were staggering, more than 20,000, dead, wounded, or missing. Thousands of the finest officers and soldiers of the South were lost on these battlefields.

The siege of Richmond was lifted and Lee emerged as a great commander.

Glory Enough for a Week

Although defeated, the army under General McClellan was still a formidable force, and was being constantly strengthened. Its proximity to the Confederate capital, and its unassailable position, the facility with which it could be transferred across James River for operations on the south side, the capacity of the North indefinitely to recruit its ranks, and of the Government to repair and increase its equipment, rendered the situation one of profound solicitude, and presented to the Confederate commander the alternative of remaining a passive observer of his adversary's movements, or of devising a campaign which would compel the withdrawal of the hostile army from its position of constant menace.

With a just conception of the inordinate fear which possessed the mind of the Federal civil authorities for the safety of their capital, he concluded that seriously to threaten that city, either by strategic manoeuvres or by a decisive blow struck at the army on its front, would be the surest way of effecting the removal of McClellan's army from its position on James River.

With this view he sent General Jackson in advance with his two divisions, followed by that of A. P. Hill, to engage General Pope, who commanded the Federal army in Northern Virginia, intending, as soon as his anticipations of the effect of this move were realized, to follow promptly with the bulk of his army.

In vindication of his sagacity, information was soon received of the transfer of troops from McClellan's army on James River to Washington.

Leaving two divisions of infantry and a brigade of cavalry at Richmond, he now moved with the rest of the army to join General Jackson, who had already presented a rebel front to the astonished gaze of Major-General John Pope, unaccustomed to such a sight, and had commenced at Cedar Run, on the 9th of August, that series of brilliant manoeuvres and engagements which so dazed the Federal commander, and so startled and alarmed the authorities at Washington.

These movements culminated with a decisive victory for the Confederates, under General Lee, over the army under General Pope, on the plains of Manassas, on the 30th of August. In the series of engagements, "more than seven thousand prisoners were taken, in addition to about two thousand wounded left in our hands. Thirty pieces of artillery, upward of twenty thousand stand of small-arms, numerous colours, and a large amount of stores, besides those taken by General Jackson at Manassas Junction, were captured."

Vanquished at Manassas, General Pope next essayed to make a stand in the fortified lines about Centreville; but another *détour* by General Jackson, under General Lee's orders, caused a further retreat in the direction of Washington, and in the early days of September the Federal army—now embracing the combined forces of McClellan and Pope—was retired within the line of fortifications constructed on the Virginia side of the river, for the protection of the Federal capital.

Outnumbered, *Pope withdraws from Warrenton Junction, August 28, 1862.*

Barely three months had elapsed since General Lee took the field, and, behold! the position of the two hostile armies, with relation to their respective seats of government, was completely reversed; fortunately for that of the North, a wide and impassable river lay between it and the victorious army of the South.

With the battles of Cedar Run, or Slaughter's Mountain, and (second) Manassas, two more victories were recorded for Confederate arms, and another Federal general was added to the list of the discomfited.

The career of General Pope was as brief and remarkable, when contrasted with his blustering proclamations, as the movements of Generals Lee and Jackson, in bringing it to a grievous termination, were audacious and brilliant.

TAYLOR, *Four Years with General Lee, pp. 57-59.*

Wrote the Rebel War Clerk:

September 1st.—Official dispatches from Lee, announcing a "signal victory," by the blessing of God, "over the combined forces of the enemy." That is glory enough for a week. When Lee says "signal victory," we know exactly what it means, and breathe freely.

There Goes Marse Robert!

Lee's repeated successes in battle brought him world-wide acclaim, and military students from many foreign countries hastened to join his armies as observers. Nothing astonished these Old World soldiers more than Lee's Spartan simplicity and the total lack of all pomp and circum-

stance in and around his encampments. In the fall of 1862 several distinguished British officers visited his camp near Winchster. In this group was Colonel Garnett Wolseley, later Commander-in-Chief of the British Army. Wolseley wrote the following account for Blackwood's Magazine, January, 1863.

Lee's headquarters consisted of about seven or eight pole-tents, pitched, with their backs to a stake-fence, upon a piece of ground so rocky that it was unpleasant to ride over it, its only recommendation being a little stream of good water which flowed close by the general's tent. In front of the tents were some three or four army-wagons, drawn up without any regularity, and a number of horses turned loose about the field. The servants—who were, of course, slaves—and the mounted soldiers called couriers, who always accompany each general of division in the field, were unprovided with tents, and slept in or under the wagons. Wagons, tents, and some of the horses were marked "U. S.", showing that part of that huge debt in the North has gone to furnishing even the Confederate generals with camp-equipments. No guard or sentries were to be seen in the vicinity, no crowd of aides-de-camp loitering about, making themselves agreeable to visitors and endeavoring to save their generals from receiving those who had no particular business. A large farm-house close by, which in any other army would have been the general's residence *pro tem;* but, as no liberties are allowed to be taken with personal property in Lee's army, he is particular in setting a good example himself. His staff are crowded together, two or three in a tent; none are allowed to carry more baggage than a small box each, and his own kit is but very little larger. Every one who approaches him does so with marked respect, although there is none of that bowing and flourishing of forage-caps which occurs in the presence of European generals; and, while all honor him and place implicit faith in his courage and ability, those with whom he is most intimate feel for him the affection of sons to a father. Old General Scott was correct in saying that when Lee joined the Southern cause it was worth as much as the accession of 20,000 men to the "rebels." Since then every injury that it was possible to inflict the Northerners have heaped upon him.

45

Notwithstanding all these personal losses, however, when speaking of the Yankees he neither evinced any bitterness of feeling nor gave utterance to a single violent expression, but alluded to many of his former friends and companions among them in the kindest terms. He spoke as a man proud of the victories won by his country and confident of ultimate success under the blessing of the Almighty, whom he glorified for past successes, and whose aid he invoked for all future operations.

Quoted in Long, *Memoirs of Robert E. Lee, pp. 228-229.*

Colonel A. L. Long, who was at that time serving on Lee's staff as military secretary, also comments on the camp near Winchester:

Notwithstanding the ruggedness of this encampment, it proved unusually lively. Besides the foreign friends, we had numerous visitors from the army, also ladies and gentlemen from Winchester and the neighborhood, all of whom had some remark to make upon the rocky situation of our camp. This the general seemed to enjoy, as it gave him an opportunity of making a jest at the expense of Colonel Long, whom he accused of having set him down there among the rocks in revenge for his refusing to occupy the yard. Although there were no habitual drinkers on the general's staff, an occasional demijohn would find its way to headquarters. While at this place one of the officers received a present of a jug of fine old rye. Soon after its advent General J. E. B. Stuart, with Sweeney and his banjo, arrived—not on account, however, of the jug, but, as was his wont, to give us a serenade. The bright camp-fire was surrounded by a merry party, and a lively concert commenced. After a while the general came out, and, observing the jug perched on a boulder, asked with a merry smile, "Gentlemen, am I to thank General Stuart or the jug for this fine music?"

By this time the men had come to know their leader. The brilliant campaigns through which he had led them had inspired them with love and confidence, and whenever he appeared among them his approach was announced by "Here comes Mars' Robert!" and he would be immediately saluted with the well-known Confederate yell, which called forth in other quarters the exclamation, "There goes Mars' Robert—old Jackson, or an ole hare."

Long, *Memoirs of Robert E. Lee, p. 229.*

Lee crosses the Potomac, *September 5-6, 1862.*

What a Cruel Thing Is War!

From Fredericksburg, Virginia, December 25, 1862, Lee wrote to his wife:

My heart is filled with gratitude to Almighty God for His unspeakable mercies with which He has blessed us in this day, for those He has granted us from the beginning of life, and particularly for those He has vouchsafed us during the past year. What should have become of us without His crowning help and protection? Oh, if our people would only recognize it and cease from self-boasting and adulation, how strong would be my belief in final success and happiness to our country! But what a cruel thing is war; to separate and destroy families and friends, and mar the purest joys and happiness God has granted us in this world; to fill our hearts with hatred instead of love for our neighbors, and to devastate the fair face of this beautiful world! I pray that, on this day when only peace and good-will are preached to mankind, better thoughts may fill the hearts of our enemies and turn them to peace. Our army was never in such good health and condition since I have been attached to it. I believe they share with me my disappointment that the enemy did not renew the combat on the 13th. I was holding back all day and husbanding our strength and ammunition for the great struggle, for which I thought I was preparing. Had I divined that was to have been his only effort, he would have had more of it. My heart bleeds at the death of every one of our gallant men.

R. E. LEE [JR.], *Recollections and Letters, pp. 88-89.*

After the second battle of Manassas, Marse Robert had taken his victorious army north into Maryland, and on September 17 at Sharpsburg he met his old adversary McClellan in what was to prove the bloodiest 12 hours fighting of the war. With vastly superior numbers McClellan forced Lee back, but on the next morning he failed to press the fight, and the Army of Northern Virginia escaped across the Potomac. Lee had hoped that his presence would bring Maryland into the Southern fold and there had also been the possibility that a successful battle waged on Union soil might bring foreign recognition and intervention. The campaign had cost many men, killed and wounded, but Lee brought back a large number of cannons and small arms from the Arsenal at Harper's Ferry.

Before the year's end, Lee was to face and defeat still another Federal Army under still another general, Ambrose E. Burnside, at Fredericksburg. The Confederates held the heights to the south of the town against repeated attacks on December 13. The defenders never budged, and the Union forces with casualties of more than 12,000 recrossed the river during the night.

I Have Lost My Right Arm

Burnside had been replaced by Major General Joseph Hooker, who was to take the Army of the Potomac on another try for Richmond. Hooker divided his forces, sending Major General John Sedgwick to demonstrate against Fredericksburg, while he led the rest of his troops to ford the Rappanannock and Rapidan, threatening Lee's rear. Greatly outnumbered, Lee left a rear guard to hold Sedgwick, and wheeled around to attack Hooker. Hooker made a stand at the crossroads known as Chancellorsville. When Stuart's cavalry brought news that the right end of the Union front terminated abruptly in the woods, Lee split his army and sent Jackson around the end of the Federal line. Jackson surprised and crushed the weak flank, but was

fatally wounded. Meanwhile, at Fredericksburg, Sedgwick attacked and carried Marye's Heights, but when Lee turned to attack Sedgwick at Salem Church, the Union armies retreated. In four days of fighting May 1-4, the Union casualties were 17,000 and the Confederates had lost 13,000. Lee against great odds had won another spectacular victory. This has been called the "high noon" of his military career. On the morning of May 3, in the words of John Esten Cooke:

The whole spectacle in the vicinity of the Chancellorsville House now in Lee's possession, was frightful. Fire, smoke, blood, confused yells, and dying groans, mingled to form the dark picture.

Lee had ridden to the front of his line, following up the enemy, and as he passed before the troops they greeted him with one prolonged, unbroken cheer, in which those wounded and lying upon the ground united. In that cheer spoke the fierce joy of men whom the hard combat had turned into blood-hounds, arousing all the ferocious instincts of the human soul. Lee sat on his horse, motionless, near the Chancellorsville House, his face and figure lit up by the glare of the burning woods, and gave his first attention, even at this exciting moment, to the unfortunates of both sides, wounded, and in danger of being burned to death. While issuing his orders on this subject, a note was brought to him from Jackson, congratulating him upon his victory. After reading it, with evidences of much emotion, he turned to the officer who had brought it and said: "Say to General Jackson that the victory is his, and that the congratulation is due to him." . . . when he received Lee's note of congratulation . . . he [Jackson] said "General Lee is very kind; but he should give the glory to God!"

. . . Jackson lay painfully, but no one supposed mortally, wounded, first at Wilderness Tavern, and then at Guiney's. Prevented from visiting the wounded man, by the responsibilities of command, now all the greater from Jackson's absence, and not regarding his hurt as serious, as indeed it did not appear to be until toward the last, Lee sent him continual messages containing good wishes and inquiries after his health. The tone of these messages is very familiar and affectionate, and leaves no doubt of the character of the relations between the two men.

"Give him my affectionate regards," he said to one officer, "and tell him to make haste and get well, and come back to me as soon as he can. He has lost his left arm, but I have lost my right."

When the wound of the great soldier took a bad turn, and it began to be whispered about that the hurt might prove fatal, Lee was strongly moved, and said with deep feeling: "Surely General Jackson must recover! God will not take him from us, now that we need him so much. Surely he will be spared to us, in answer to the many prayers which are offered for him!"

He paused after uttering these words, laboring evidently under very deep and painful emotion. After remaining silent for some moments, he added: "When you return I trust you will find him better. When a suitable occasion offers, give him my love, and tell him that I wrestled in prayer for him last night, as I have never prayed, I believe, for myself."

.   .   .   .

Jackson died on the 10th of May, and the unexpected intelligence shocked Lee profoundly. He mourned the death of the illustrious soldier with a sorrow too deep almost to find relief in tears; and issued a general order to the troops, which was in the following words:

"With deep grief the commanding general announces to the army the death of Lieutenant-General T. J. Jackson, who expired on the 10th inst., at quarter-past three P.M. The daring, skill, and energy of this great and good soldier, by the decree of an All-wise Providence, are now lost to us. But, while we mourn his death, we feel that his spirit still lives, and will inspire the whole army with his indomitable courage and unshaken confidence in God, as our hope and strength. Let his name be a watchword to his corps, who have followed him to victory on so many fields. Let his officers and soldiers emulate his invincible determination to do everything in defence of our beloved country."

JOHN ESTEN COOKE, *A Life of General Robert E. Lee, pp. 245, 265-268.*

Lee on Traveller *in battle, 1863. From a colored engraving by an unknown artist. Courtesy, Confederate Museum, Richmond, Va.*

Peace Might Be the Best Way Out

In the midst of preparations for the expedition to Pennsylvania, Lee wrote a most significant communication to President Davis. In it he urged that every encouragement be given to the rising peace party in the North. It is improbable that Lee really believed that the war could be terminated satisfactorily to the South by such means, but it is interesting to note that almost two years before Appomattox, he foresaw the end.

Headquarters Army of Northern Virginia,
June 10, 1863.

His Excellency Jefferson Davis, Richmond:

Mr. President: I beg leave to bring to your attention a subject with reference to which I have thought that the course pursued by writers and speakers among us has had a tendency to interfere with our success. I refer to the manner in which the demonstration of a desire for peace at the North has been received in our country.

I think there can be no doubt that journalists and others at the South, to whom the Northern people naturally look for a reflection of our opinions, have met these indications in such wise as to weaken the hands of the advocates of a pacific policy on the part of the Federal Government, and give much encouragement to those who urge a continuance of the war.

Recent political movements in the United States, and the comments of influential newspapers upon them, have attracted my attention particularly to this subject, which I deem not unworthy of the consideration of Your Excellency, nor inappropriate to be adverted to by me, in view of its connection with the situation of military affairs.

Conceding to our enemies the superiority claimed by them in numbers, resources, and all the means and appliances for carrying on the war, we have no right to look for exemptions from the military consequences of a vigorous use of these advantages, excepting by such deliverance as the mercy of Heaven may accord to the courage of our soldiers, the justice of our cause, and the constancy and prayers of our people. While making the most we can of the means of resistance we possess, and gratefully accepting the measure of success with which God has blessed our efforts as an earnest of His approval and favor, it is nevertheless the part of wisdom to carefully measure and husband our strength, and not to expect from it more than in the ordinary course of affairs it is capable of accomplishing. We should not, therefore, conceal from ourselves that our resources in men are constantly diminishing, and the disproportion in this respect between us and our enemies, if they continue united in their efforts to subjugate us, is steadily augmenting.

The decrease of the aggregate of this army, as disclosed by the returns, affords an illustration of this fact. Its effective strength varies from time to time, but the falling off in its aggregate shows that the ranks are growing weaker and that its losses are not supplied by recruits.

Under these circumstances, we should neglect no honorable means of dividing and weakening our enemies, that they may feel some of the difficulties experienced by ourselves. It seems to me that the most effectual mode of accomplishing this object, now within our reach, is to give all the encouragement we can, consistently with truth, to the rising peace party of the North.

Nor do I think we should, in this connection, make nice distinction between those who declare for peace unconditionally and those who advocate it as a means of restoring the Union, however much we may prefer the former.

We should bear in mind that the friends of peace at the North must make concessions to the earnest desire that exists in the minds of their countrymen for a restoration of the Union, and that to hold out such a result as an inducement is essential to the success of their party.

Should the belief that peace will bring back the Union become general, the war would no longer be supported, and that, after all, is what we are interested in bringing about. When peace is proposed to us, it will be time enough to discuss its terms, and it is not the part of prudence to spurn the proposition in advance, merely because those who wish to make it believe, or affect to believe, that it will result in bringing us back to the Union. We entertain no such apprehensions, nor doubt that the desire of our people for a distinct and independent national existence will prove as steadfast under the influence of peaceful measures as it has shown itself in the midst of war.

If the views I have indicated meet the approval of Your Excellency, you will best know how to give effect to them. Should you deem them inexpedient or impracticable, I think you will nevertheless agree with me that we should at least carefully abstain from measures or expressions that tend to discourage any party whose purpose is peace.

With the statement of my opinion on the subject, the length of which you will excuse, I leave to your better judgement to determine the proper course to be pursued.

I am, with great respect, your obedient servant,

R. E. Lee, *General.*

Official Records, 27, part 3, pp. 880-882.

We Had Much Need of Borrowing Supplies

After the smashing victory at Chancellorsville, Lee determined to take his army across the Potomac to the rich farm lands of Pennsylvania. On June 3 he started his long line moving first northwestward across the Blue Ridge, then northward in the Shenandoah Valley. The army was comprised of three infantry corps under James Longstreet, A. P. Hill, and R. S. Ewell, and a cavalry division under J. E. B. Stuart. Once across the Potomac, Lee's first objective was Harrisburg, and the Confederates were to proceed in two columns, one by the Chambersburg route, the other by way of Emmitsburg. Rodes's division of Ewell's corps reached Carlisle on June 27. Early's command of 8,000 men, also a part of Ewell's corps, passed through Gettysburg on June 26 and reached the Susquehanna at York on June 28. General John B. Gordon, who held a command under Early, analyzes this most significant campaign of the Civil War.

From Gettysburg to Appomattox; from the zenith of assurance to the nadir of despair; from the compact ranks, boundless confidence, and exultant hopes of as proud and puissant an army as was ever marshalled—to the shattered remnants, withered hopes, and final surrender of that army—such is the track to be followed describing the Confederacy's declining fortunes and ultimate death. No picture can be drawn by human hand vivid enough to portray the varying hues, the spasmodic changes, the rapidly gathering shadows of the scenes embraced in the culminating period of the great struggle.

A brief analysis of the reasons for General Lee's crossing of the Potomac is now in order. In the logistics of defensive war, offensive movements are often the wisest strategy. Voltaire has somewhere remarked that "to subsist one's army at the expense of the enemy, to advance on their own ground and force them to retrace their steps—thus rendering strength useless by skill—is regarded as one of the masterpieces of military art."

. . . while the movement into Maryland in 1862, and into Pennsylvania in 1863, were each defensive in design, they differed in some particulars as to the immediate object which General Lee hoped to accomplish. Each sought to force the Union army to retrace its steps; "each sought to render strength useless by skill;" but in 1862 there was not so grave a necessity for subsisting his army on Union soil as in 1863. The movement into Maryland was of course a more direct threat upon Washington. Besides, at that period there was still a prevalent belief among Southern leaders that Southern sentiment was strong in Maryland, and that an important victory within her borders might convert the Confederate camps into recruiting-stations, and add materially to the strength of Lee's army. But the Confederate graves which were dug in Maryland's soil vastly outnumbered the Confederate soldiers recruited from her citizens. . . .

The movement into Pennsylvania in 1863 was also, in part at least, a recruiting expedition. We did not expect, it is true, to gather soldiers for our ranks, but beeves for our commissary. For more than two years the effort to fill the ranks of the Southern armies had alarmingly reduced the ranks of Southern producers, with no appreciable diminution in the number of consumers. Indeed, the consumers had materially increased; for while we were not then seeking to encourage Northern immigration, we had a large number of visitors from that and other sections, who were exploring the country under such efficient guides as McClellan, Hooker, Grant, Sherman, Thomas, and others. We had, therefore, much need of borrowing supplies from our neighbors beyond the Potomac. . . .

Again, to defend Richmond by threatening Washington and Baltimore and Philadelphia was perhaps the most promising purpose of the Confederate invasion. Incidentally, it was hoped that a defeat of the Union army in territory so contiguous to these great cities would send gold to such a premium as to cause financial panic in the commercial centres, and induce the great business interests to demand that the war should cease. But the hoped-for victory, with its persuasive influence, did not materialize. Indeed, the presence of Lee's army in Pennsylvania seemed to arouse the North to still greater efforts, as the presence of the Union armies in the South had intensified, if possible, the decision of her people to resist to the last extremity.

GENERAL JOHN B. GORDON, *Reminiscences of the Civil War, pp. 137-140.*

Take Care Madam

In retrospect it is not too difficult to put together a coherent description of a great military campaign and battle, but at the time these events were taking place they were often confusing to the individual observer and sometimes incomprehensible. On June 20th, 1863, a British officer, Lieutenant-Colonel A. J. L. Fremantle, of the Coldstream Guards, left Richmond, Virginia, to join the Confederate army. He was armed with letters from the Secretary-of-War for Generals Lee and Longstreet. Fremantle kept a daily diary and through his eyes, notwithstanding his bias toward the South, we can join in spirit those men in grey who marched so gaily northward to the tune of "Dixie's Land," one hundred years ago.

Twenty-second June (Monday).—We started without food or corn at 6:30 A. M., and soon became entangled with Pender's Division on its line of march, which delayed us a good deal. . . .

The soldiers of this division are a remarkably fine body of men, and look quite seasoned and ready for any work. Their clothing is serviceable, so also are their boots; but there is the usual utter absence of uniformity as to colour and shape of their garments and hats: grey of all shades, and brown clothing, with felt hats predominate. The Confederate troops are now entirely armed with excellent rifles, most Enfields. . . .

25th June (Thursday) The weather was cool and showery, and all went swimmingly for the first fourteen miles, when we caught up McLaw's division, which belongs to Longstreet's corps. . . . They were commanded, I think, by Semmes and Barksdale, and were composed of Georgians, Mississippians, and South Carolinians. They marched very well, and there was no attempt at straggling; quite a different state of things from Johnston's men in Mississippi. All were well shod and efficiently clothed. In rear of each regiment were from twenty to thirty negro slaves, and a certain number of unarmed men carrying stretchers and wearing in their hats the red badges of the ambulance corps; — this is an excellent institution, for it prevents unwounded men falling out on pretence of taking wounded to the rear. The knapsacks of the men still bear the names of the Massachusetts, Vermont, New Jersey, or other regiments to which they originally belonged. There were about twenty waggons to each brigade, most of which were marked U. S., and each of these brigades was about 2800 strong. There were four brigades in McLaw's division. All the men seemed in the highest spirits, and were cheering and yelling most vociferously.

27th June (Saturday) After riding eight miles, I came up with General Longstreet, at 6:30 A.M. . . . He told me (which I did not know) that we were now in Pennsylvania, the enemy's country—Maryland being only ten miles broad at this point. . . . Whilst speaking of entering upon the enemy's soil, he said to me that although it might be fair in just retaliation, *to apply the torch*, yet that doing so would demoralize the army and ruin its now excellent discipline. Private property is therefore to be rigidly protected.

I rode slowly on to rejoin General Longstreet, near Chambersburg, which is a Pennsylvania town, distant twenty-two miles from Hagerstown. I was with M'Law's division, and observed that the moment they entered Pennsylvania, the troops opened the fences and enlarged the road about twenty yards on each side, which enabled the wagons and themselves to proceed together. This is the only damage I saw done by the Confederates. . . .

In passing through Greencastle we found all the houses and windows shut up, the natives in their Sunday clothes standing at their doors regarding the troops in a very unfriendly manner. I saw no straggling into the houses, nor were any of the inhabitants disturbed or annoyed by the soldiers. Sentries were placed at the doors of many of the best houses, to prevent any officer or soldier from getting in on any pretense.

I entered Chambersburg at 6 P.M. This is a town of some size and importance. All its houses were shut up; but the natives were in the streets, or at the upper windows, looking in a scowling and bewildered manner at the Confederate troops, who were marching gaily past to the tune of Dixie's Land. The women (many of whom were pretty and well dressed) were particularly sour and disagreeable in their remarks. I heard one of them say, "Look at Pharaoh's army going to the Red Sea." Others were pointing and laughing at Hood's ragged Jacks, who were passing at the time. This division, well known for its fighting qualities, is composed of Texans, Alabamians, and Arkansians, and they certainly are a queer lot to look at. They carry less than any other troops; many of them have only got an old piece of carpet or rug as baggage; many have discarded their shoes in the mud; all are ragged and dirty, but full of good humor and confidence in themselves and in their general, Hood. They answered the numerous taunts of the Chambersburg ladies with cheers and laughter. One female had seen fit to adorn her ample bosom with a huge Yankee flag, and she stood at the door of her house, her countenance expressing the greatest contempt for the barefooted Rebs; several companies passed her without taking any notice; but at length a Texan gravely remarked, "Take care, Madam, for Hood's boys are great at storming breastworks, when the Yankee colours is on them." After this speech the patriotic lady beat a precipitate retreat.

LT. COL. A. J. L. FREMANTLE, *Three Months in the States, April- June, 1863, pp. 114 et seq.*

A Bouquet for General Gordon

Early's division had reached the Susquehanna and expected to cross the river over the bridge at Columbia in order to approach Harrisburg from the east.

General Gordon again takes up the narrative:

We entered the city of York on Sunday morning. A committee, composed of the mayor and prominent citizens, met my command on the main pike before we reached the corporate limits, their object being to make a peaceable surrender and ask for protection to life and property. They returned, I think, with a feeling of assured safety. The church bells were ringing, and the streets were filled with well-dressed people. The appearance of these church-going men, women, and children, in their Sunday attire, strangely contrasted with that of my marching soldiers. Begrimed as we were from head to foot with the impalpable gray powder which rose in dense columns from the macadamized pikes and settled in sheets on men, horses, and wagons, it is no wonder that many of York's inhabitants were terror-stricken as they looked upon us. We had been compelled on these forced marches to leave baggage-wagons behind us, and there was no possibility of a change of clothing, an no time for brushing uniforms or washing the disfiguring dust from faces, hair, or beard. All these were of the same hideous hue. The grotesque aspect of my troops was accentuated here and there, too, by barefooted men mounted double upon huge horses with shaggy manes and long fetlocks. Confederate pride, to say nothing of Southern gallantry, was subjected to the sorest trial by the consternation produced among the ladies of York. . . .

As we moved along the street . . . a little girl, probably twelve years of age, ran up to my horse and handed me a large bouquet of flowers, in the centre of which was a note, in delicate handwriting, purporting to give the numbers and describe the position of the Union forces of Wrightsville, toward which I was advancing. I carefully read and reread this strange note. It bore no signature, and contained no assurance of sympathy for the Southern cause, but it was so terse and explicit in its terms as to compel my confidence. The second day we were in front of Wrightsville, and from the high ridge on which this note suggested that I halt and examine the position of the Union troops, I eagerly scanned the prospect with my field-glasses, in order to verify the truth of the mysterious communication or detect its misrepresentations. There, in full view before us, was the town, just as described, nestling on the banks of the Susquehanna. There was the blue line of soldiers guarding the approach, drawn up, as indicated, along an intervening ridge and across the pike. There was the long bridge spanning the Susquehanna and connecting the town with Columbia on the other bank. Most important of all, there was the deep gorge or ravine running off to the right and extending around the left flank of the Federal line and to the river below the bridge. Not an inaccurate detail in that note could be discovered. I did not hesitate, therefore, to adopt its suggestion of moving down the gorge in order to throw my command on the flank, or possibly in the rear, of the Union troops and force them to a rapid retreat or surrender. . . .

GORDON, *Reminiscences of the Civil War, pp. 142-144.*

Lee's converging movement on Harrisburg seemed to be on the eve of success, when an unforeseen shift of events between June 25 and June 28 threatened to wipe out every advantage he had gained thus far in his daring march up the Shenandoah and Cumberland Valleys. Lee's bold move had been discovered by the Federals. Gen. George G. Meade replaced Hooker with orders to assume command of the army at Frederick, Maryland, on June 28. Meanwhile, General Stuart, with the Confederate cavalry, operating in the rear of the Union army, was in eastern Maryland on June 28, wholly out of touch with the Confederate force. Lee was thus without eyes or ears at a time he needed them most.

On the night of June 28, Lee learned that the Federal forces had crossed the Potomac and were in the vicinity of Frederick, Maryland. With the entire Union Army close at hand and with many miles between him and his base, Lee decided to abandon his original plan and to concentrate for battle. He moved his army at once across the mountains to Cashtown, 8 miles from Gettysburg. Here, near Cashtown, he planned to establish his battle position. Rodes, then at Carlisle, and Early, at York were at once ordered to this point.

Handsomest Man of His Age

On the eve of battle British Colonel Fremantle met Lee for the first time. In his diary he wrote:

hirtieth June (Tuesday)—This morning, before marching from Chambersburg, General Longstreet introduced me to the Commander-in-Chief. General Lee is, almost without exception, the handsomest man of his age I ever saw. He is fifty-six years old, tall, broadshouldered, very well made, well set-up—a thorough soldier in appearance; and his manners are most courteous and full of dignity. He is a perfect gentleman in every respect. I imagine no man has so few enemies, or is so universally esteemed. Throughout the South, all agree in pronouncing him to be as near perfection as a man can be. He has none of the small vices, such as smoking, drinking, chewing, or swearing, and his bitterest enemy never accused him of the greater ones. He generally wears a well-worn long gray jacket, a high black felt hat, and blue trousers tucked into his Wellington boots. I never saw him carry arms; and the only mark of his military rank are the three stars on his collar. He rides a handsome horse, which is extremely well groomed. He himself is very neat in his dress and person, and in the most arduous marches he always looks smart and clean. [Footnote]: I observed this during the three days' fighting at Gettysburg, and in the retreat afterwards, when everyone else looked, and was extremely dirty.

I Wouldn't Have Missed This for Anything!

Colonel Fremantle, as a foreign observer had the run of the battlefield. Sometimes he was mounted, sometimes afoot. He covered an amazing amount of territory and took desperate chances. His narrative of the great battle is necessarily confused, but at the same time it is vigorous and vivid in descriptive power.

First July (Wednesday)—We did not leave our camp till noon, as nearly all General Hill's corps had to pass our quarters on its march towards Gettysburg. . . .

At 2 P.M. firing became distinctly audible in our front, but although it increased as we progressed, it did not seem to be very heavy.

At 3 P.M. we began to meet wounded men coming to the rear, and the number of these soon increased most rapidly, some hobbling alone, others on stretchers carried by the ambulance corps, and others in the ambulance waggons. Many of the latter were stripped nearly naked, and displayed very bad wounds. This spectacle, so revolting to a person unaccustomed to such sights, produced no impression whatever upon the advancing troops, who certainly go under fire with the most perfect nonchalence; they show no enthusiasm or excitement, but the most complete indifference. This is the effect of two years' almost uninterrupted fighting.

We now began to meet Yankee prisoners coming to the rear in considerable numbers. Many of them were wounded, but they seemed already to be on excellent terms with their captors, with whom they had commenced swapping canteens, tobacco, &c. . . . In answer to a question, I heard one of them remark, with a laugh, "We're pretty nigh whipped already." We next came to a Confederate soldier carrying a Yankee color, belonging, I think, to a Pennsylvania regiment, which he told me he had just captured.

At 4:30 P.M. we came in sight of Gettysburg and joined General Lee and General Hill, who were on the top of one of the ridges which form the peculiar feature of the country round Gettysburg. We could see the enemy retreating up one of the opposite ridges, pursued by the Confederates with loud yells. The position into which the enemy had been driven was evidently a strong one. His right appeared to rest on an cemetery, on the top of a high ridge to the right of Gettysburg, as we looked at it.

The firing ceased about dark, at which time I rode back with General Longstreet and his Staff to his headquarters at Cashtown, a little village eight miles from Gettysburg. At that time troops were pouring along the road, and were being marched towards the position they are to occupy tomorrow.

In the fight to-day nearly 6,000 prisoners had been taken, and 10 guns. . . . This day's

Louisiana Tigers *attack a battery of the 11th Corps at Gettysburg, July 1, 1863.*

work is called a "brisk little scurry," and all anticipate a "big battle" tomorrow.

I observed that the artillery-men in charge of the horses dig themselves little holes like graves, throwing up the earth at the upper end. They ensconce themselves in these holes when under fire.

At supper this evening, General Longstreet spoke of the enemy's position as being "very formidable." He also said that they would doubtless intrench themselves strongly during the night. [Note]: *I have the best reason for supposing that the fight came off prematurely, and that neither Lee nor Longstreet intended that it should have begun that day. I also think that their plans were deranged by the events of the first.* The Staff officers spoke of the battle as a certainty, and the universal feeling in the army was one of profound contempt for an enemy whom they have beaten so constantly, and under so many disadvantages.

2nd July (Thursday) At 7 A.M. I rode over part of the ground with General Longstreet, and saw him disposing McLaw's division for to-day's fight. The enemy occupied a series of high ridges, the tops of which were covered with trees, but the intervening valleys between their ridges and ours were mostly open, and partly under cultivation. The cemetery was on their right, and their left appeared to rest upon a high rocky hill. The enemy's forces, which were now supposed to comprise nearly the whole Potomac army, were concentrated into a space apparently not more than a couple of miles in length. The Confederates inclosed them in a sort of semicircle, and the extreme extent of our position must have been from five to six miles at least. Ewell was on our left; his headquarters in a church (with a high cupola) at Gettysburg; Hill in the centre; and Longstreet on the right. Our ridges were also covered with pine-woods at the tops, and generally on the rear slopes. The artillery of both sides confronted each other at the edges of these belts of trees, the troops being completely hidden. The enemy was evidently intrenched, but the Southerners had not broken ground at all. A dead silence reigned until 4:45 P.M., and no one would have imagined that such masses of men and such a powerful artillery were about to commence the work of destruction at that hour.

. . . And we began to doubt whether a fight was coming off to-day at all. At that time, however, Longstreet suddenly commenced a heavy cannonade on the right. Ewell immediately took it up on the left. The enemy replied with at least equal fury, and in a few moments the firing along the whole line was as heavy as it is possible to conceive. . . .

So soon as the firing began, General Lee joined Hill just below our tree, and he remained there nearly all the time, looking through his field-glass—sometimes talking to Hill and sometimes to Colonel Long of his Staff. But generally he sat quite alone on the stump of a tree. What I remarked especially was, that during the whole time the firing continued, he only sent one message, and only received one report. It is evidently his system to arrange the plan thoroughly with the three corps commanders, and then leave to them the duty of modifying and carrying it out to the best of their abilities.

When the cannonade was at its height, a Confederate band of music, between the cemetery and ourselves, began to play polkas and waltzes, which sounded very curious, accompanied by the hissing and bursting of the shells.

At 5:45 all became comparatively quiet on our left and in the cemetery; but volleys of musketry on the right told us that Longstreet's infantry were advancing, and the onward progress of the smoke showed that he was progressing favourably; but about 6:30 there seemed to be a check, and even a slight retrograde movement. Soon after 7, General Lee got a report by signal from Longstreet to say *"we are doing well. . . ."*

3rd July (Friday) We joined Generals Lee and Longstreet's Staff: they were reconnoitering and making preparations for renewing the attack. . . .

The plan of yesterday's attack seems to have been very simple—first a heavy cannonade all along the line, followed by an advance of Longstreet's two divisions and part of Hill's corps. In consequence of the enemy's having been driven back some distance, Longstreet's corps (part of it) was in a much more forward situation than yesterday. But the range of heights to be gained was still most formidable, and evidently strongly entrenched.

The distance between the Confederate guns and the Yankee position—i.e., between the woods crowning the opposite ridges—was at least a mile—quite open, gently undulating, and exposed to artillery the whole distance. This was the ground which had to be crossed in to-day's attack. Pickett's division, which has just come up, was to bear the brunt in Longstreet's attack, together with Heth and Pettigrew in Hill's corps. Pickett's division was a weak one (under 5,000), owing to the absence of two brigades.

At noon all Longstreet's dispositions were made; his troops for attack were deployed into line, and lying down in the woods; his batteries were ready to open. The General then dismounted and went to sleep for a short time. . . . I now rode off to get, if possible, into some commanding position from whence we could see the whole thing without being exposed to the tremendous fire which was about to commence. . . .

Not finding such a safe vantage point, Fremantle decided about 2:30 o'clock to make his way back to Longstreet.

After passing General Lee and his Staff, I rode on through the woods in the direction in which I had left Longstreet. I soon began to meet many wounded men returning from the front; many of them asked in piteous tones the way to a doctor or an ambulance. The further I got, the greater became the number of the wounded. At last I came to a perfect stream of them flocking through the woods in numbers as great as the crowd in Oxford-street in the middle of day. Some were walking along on crutches composed of two rifles, others were supported by men less badly wounded than themselves, and others were carried on stretchers by the ambulance corps; but in no case did I see a sound man helping the wounded to the rear, unless he carried the red badge of the ambulance corps. They were still under a heavy fire; the shells were continually bringing down great limbs of trees, and carrying further destruction amongst this melancholy procession. I saw all this in much less time than it takes to write it, and although astonished to meet such vast numbers of wounded, I had not seen *enough* to give me an idea of the real extent of the mischief.

When I got close up to General Longstreet, I saw one of his regiments advancing through the woods in good order; so, thinking I was just in the time to see the attack, I remarked to the General that *"I wouldn't have missed this for anything."* Longstreet was seated at the top of a snake fence at the edge of the wood, and looking perfectly calm and imperturbed. He replied, laughing, "The devil you wouldn't! *I would like to have missed it very much; we've attacked and been repulsed: look there!"*

For the first time I then had a view of the open space between the two positions, and saw it covered with Confederates slowly and sulkily returning towards us in small broken parties, under a heavy fire of artillery. But the fire where we were was not so bad as further to the rear; for although the air seemed alive with shell, yet the greater number burst behind us.

The General told me that Pickett's division had succeeded in carrying the enemy's position and capturing his guns, but after remaining there twenty minutes, it had been forced to retire, on the retreat of Heth and Pettigrew on its left. No person could have been more calm or self-possessed than General Longstreet under these trying circumstances, aggravated as they now were by the movements of the enemy, who began to show a strong disposition to advance. I could now thoroughly appreciate the term bulldog, which I had heard applied to him by the soldiers. Difficulties seem to make no other impression upon him than to make him a little more savage.

If Longstreet's conduct was admirable, that of General Lee was perfectly sublime. He was engaged in rallying and in encouraging the broken troops, and was riding about a little in front of the wood, quite alone—the whole of his staff being engaged in a similar manner further to the rear. His face, which is always placid and cheerful, did not show signs of the slightest disappointment, care, or annoyance; and he was addressing to every soldier he met a few words of encouragement, such as, "All this will come right in the end; we'll talk it over afterwards, but, in the meantime, all good men must rally. We want all good and true men just now, &c. He spoke to all the wounded men that passed him,

and the slightly wounded he exhorted, "to bind up their hurts and take up a musket" in this emergency. Very few failed to answer his appeal, and I saw many badly wounded men take off their hats and cheer him. He said to me, "This has been a sad day for us, Colonel—a sad day; but we can't expect always to gain victories." He was also kind enough to advise me to get into some more sheltered position, as the shells were bursting round us with considerable frequency.

Notwithstanding the misfortune which had so suddenly befallen him, General Lee seemed to observe everything, however trivial. When a mounted officer began licking his horse for shying at the bursting of a shell, he called out, "Don't whip him, Captain; don't whip him. I've got just such another foolish horse myself, and whipping does no good."

I happened to see a man lying flat on his face in a small ditch, and I remarked that I didn't think he seemed dead; this drew General Lee's attention to the man, who commenced groaning dismally. Finding appeals to his patriotism of no avail, General Lee had him ignominiously set on his legs by some neighboring gunners.

I saw General Willcox (an officer who wears a short round jacket and a battered straw hat) come to him, and explain, almost crying, the state of his brigade. General Lee immediately shook hands with him and said cheerfully, "Never mind, General, *all this has been MY fault*—it is *I* that have lost this fight, and you must help me out of it in the best way you can. . . ."

FREMANTLE, Three Months in the the Southern States, pp. 125-135.

High Water Mark of the Rebellion

Whatever differences of opinion may now or hereafter exist as to the results which might have followed a defeat of the Union arms at Gettysburg, there is universal concurrence in the judgment that this battle was the turning-point in the South's fortunes. The point where Pickett's Virginians, under Kemper, Garnett, and Armistead, in their immortal charge, swept over the rock wall, has been appropriately designated by the Government as "the high-water mark of the Rebellion." To the Union commander, General George Gordon Meade, history will accord the honor of having handled his army at Gettysburg with unquestioned ability. The record and the results of the battle entitle him to a high place among Union leaders. To him and to his able subordinates and heroic men is due the credit of having successfully met and repelled the Army of Northern Virginia in the meridian of its hope and confidence and power. This much seems secure to him, whether his failure vigorously to follow General Lee and force him to another battle is justified or condemned by the military critics of the future. General Meade's army halted, it is true, after having achieved a victory. . . .

GORDON, Reminiscences of the Civil War, p. 158.

Four Wheel Carriage With a Harmless Load of Females

It is interesting to speculate on what might have happened had Meade mounted an attack on the retreating columns of Lee. The Confederates were slowed down by muddy roads and between them and Virginia lay the Potomac with waters swollen by heavy rains. Colonel Fremantle accompanied the retreating army as far as Hagerstown where he obtained a pass through the Union lines in order that he might return to England. His diary contains a vivid record of the long march back to the river.

ourth July (Saturday) [1863] . . . the army is to commence moving in the direction of Virginia this evening. This step is imperative from want of ammunition. But it was hoped that the enemy might attack during the day, especially as this is the 4th of July, and it was calculated that there was still ammunition for one day's fighting. The ordnance train had already commenced moving back towards Cashtown, and Ewell's immense train of plunder had been proceeding towards Hagerstown by the Fairfield road ever since an early hour this morning.

At 1 P.M. the rain began to descend in torrents, and we took refuge in the hovel of an ignorant Pennsylvania boor. The cottage was full of soldiers, none of whom had the slightest idea of the contemplated retreat, and were all talking of Washington and Baltimore with the greatest confidence.

At 2 P.M. we walked to General Longstreet's camp, which had been removed to a place three miles distant, on the Fairfield road. . . .

Wagons, horses, mules, and cattle captured in Pennsylvania, the solid advantages of this campaign, have been passing slowly along this road (Fairfield) all day; those taken by Ewell are particularly admired. So interminable was this train that it soon became evident that we should not be able to start till late at night.. As soon as it became dark we all lay round a big fire, and I heard reports coming in from the different generals that the enemy was *retiring,* and had been doing so all day long. . . .

5th July (Sunday).—The night was very bad—thunder and lightning, torrents of rain —the road knee deep in mud and water, and often blocked up with waggons "come to grief." I pitied the wretched plight of the unfortunate soldiers who were to follow us. Our progress was naturally very slow indeed, and we took eight hours to go as many miles.

At 8 A.M. we halted a little beyond the village of Fairfield, near the entrance to a mountain pass. No sooner had we done so and lit a fire, than an alarm was spread that Yankee cavalry were upon us. . . . Soon afterwards some Confederate cavalry were pushed to the front, who cleared the pass after a slight skirmish.

The road was full of soldiers marching in a particularly lively manner—the wet and mud seemed to have produced no effect whatever on their spirits, which were as boisterous as ever. . . .

We all slept in the open, and the heavy rain produced no effect upon our slumbers.

6th July (Monday)—A short time before we reached Hagerstown there was some firing in front, together with an alarm that the Yankee cavalry was upon us. The ambulances were sent back; but some of the wounded jumped out, and, producing the rifles which they had not parted with, they prepared to fight. After a good deal of desultory skirmishing, we seated ourselves upon a hill overlooking Hagerstown, and saw the enemy's cavalry driven through the town pursued by yelling Confederates. A good many Yankee prisoners now passed us; one of them, who was smoking a cigar, was a lieutenant of cavalry, dressed very smartly, and his hair brushed with the greatest care; he formed rather a contrast to his ragged escort, and to ourselves, who had not washed or shaved for ever so long.

About 7 P.M. we rode through Hagerstown . . . proceeding about a mile beyond the town we halted, and General Longstreet sent four cavalrymen up a lane, with directions to report everything they saw. We then dismounted and lay down. About ten minutes later (being nearly dark) we heard a sudden rush—a panic—and then a regular stampede commenced, in the midst of which I descried our four cavalry heroes crossing a field as fast as they could gallop. All was now complete confusion;—officers mounting their horses, and pursuing those which had got loose, and soldiers climbing over fences for protection against the supposed advanced Yankees. In the middle of the din I heard an artillery officer shouting to his "cannoneers" to stand by him, and plant the guns in a proper position for enfilading the lane. I also distinguished Longstreet walking about, hustled by the excited crowd, and remarking, in angry tones, which could scarcely be heard, and to which no attention was paid, "Now, you don't know what it is—you don't know what it is." Whilst the row and confusion were at their height, the object of all this alarm at length emerged from the dark lane, in the shape of a domestic four-wheel carriage, with a harmless load of females. The stampede had, however, spread, increased in the rear, and caused much harm and delay.

Cavalry skirmishing went on until quite dark, a determined attack having been made by the enemy, who did his best to prevent the trains from crossing the Potomac at Williamsport. It resulted in the success of the Confederates. . . .

FREMANTLE, Three Months in the Southern States, pp. 138 ff.

I Am Alone to Blame

From Hagerstown, Maryland, on July 12, 1863, Lee wrote his wife:

You will . . . learn before this reaches you that our success at Gettysburg was not so great as reported—in fact, that we failed to drive the enemy from his position, and that our army withdrew to the Potomac. . . .

And from Bunker Hill on July 15, he again wrote his wife:

The army has returned to Virginia. Its return is rather sooner than I had originally contemplated. . . .

R. E. LEE [JR.], Recollections and Letters, pp. 101, 108.

To President Davis, from Camp Culpepper, July 31, Lee reported:

No blame can be attached to the army for its failure to accomplish what was projected by me, nor should it be censored for the unreasonable expectations of the public—I am alone to blame, in perhaps expecting too much of its prowess & valor. It however in my opinion achieved under the guidance of the Most High a general success, though it did not win a victory. I thought at the time that the latter was practicable. I still think if all things could have worked together it would have been accomplished. But with the knowledge I then had, & in the circumstances I was then placed, I do not know what better course I could have pursued. With my present knowledge, & could I have foreseen that the attack on the last day would have failed to drive the enemy from his position, I should certainly have tried some other course. What the ultimate result would have been is not so clear to me. Our loss has been very heavy, that of the enemys is proportionately so. His crippled condition enabled us to retire from the Country, comparatively unmolested. . .

DOUGLAS SOUTHALL FREEMAN, Lee's Dispatches, p. 110.

Five years later in 1868, in a letter to Major William McDonald, of Berryville, Clarke County, Virginia, who was intending to write a school history, Lee made the following statement:

As to the battle of Gettysburg, I must again refer you to the official accounts. Its loss was occasioned by a combination of circumstances. It was commenced in the absence of correct intelligence. It was continued in the effort to overcome the difficulties by which we were surrounded, and it would have been gained could one determined and united blow have delivered by our whole line. As it was, victory trembled in the balance for three days, and the battle resulted in the infliction of as great an amount of injury as was received and in frustrating the Federal campaign for the season.

R. E. LEE [JR.], Recollections and Letters, p. 102.

IV. BY ACCIDENT, LEE BEAT US
TO SPOTSYLVANIA

In March, 1864, Lincoln gave Grant command of all Union armies and the stage was set for the two giants of the Civil War, Lee and Grant, to meet in combat. Grant turned over his western army to Sherman and joined Meade in Virginia. There were then five principal Union armies; two big ones, Meade's and Sherman's; and three smaller ones, Sigel's in the Shenandoah, Butler's on the James River south of Richmond, and Bank's operating west of the Mississippi on the Red River.

In May, Sherman started down the railroad from Chattanooga to Atlanta and Grant, with Meade, crossed the Rapidan west of Chancellorsville. Grant's objective was to annihilate the Army of Northern Virginia and to capture the Confederate capital. Lee did not wait to be attacked, but moved promptly to meet the Army of the Potomac in the heavy forest area known as the Wilderness. His mission was to prevent the capture of Richmond and, if possible, to destroy Grant or force him to retreat.

In the forty days of this campaign, with a two to one superiority over Lee, with unlimited supplies, munitions, and reserves, Grant advanced to the south side of the James River and forced Lee to fall back from the Rapidan to Richmond. The Union losses in killed, wounded, and captured were appalling. The Southern losses, while fewer, were more damaging. Grant failed to achieve his objective, the capture of Richmond, but he drove the unbeaten army of Lee from the open field to the security of fixed fortifications.

Throughout this campaign Grant underestimated the generalship of Lee and the fighting capacity of the ragged Rebel army.

In breaking off the fight in the Wilderness after he was outflanked by Lee, Grant said:

My object in moving to Spotsylvania was two fold: first, I did not want Lee to get back to Richmond in time to attempt to crush Butler before I could get there; second, I wanted to get between his army and Richmond if possible; and, if not, to draw him into the open field. But Lee, by accident, beat us to Spotsylvania.

GRANT, Personal Memoirs, Vol. II, p. 211.

On the morning of May 11, Grant wrote Major General H. W. Halleck, his chief of staff:

We have now ended the sixth day of very heavy fighting. The result to this time is much in our favor. But our losses have been heavy, as well as those of the enemy. We have lost to this time 11 general officers, killed, wounded, and missing, and probably 20,000 men. I think the loss of the enemy must be greater, we having taken over 4,000 prisoners in battle, while he has taken but few, except stragglers. I am now sending back to Belle Plain all my wagons for a fresh supply of provisions and ammunition, and propose to fight it out on this line if it takes all summer.

The arrival of re-enforcements here will be very encouraging to the men, and I hope they will be sent as fast as possible, and in as great numbers. . . . I am satisfied the enemy are shaky, and are only kept up to the mark by the greatest exertions on the part of their officers, and by keeping them intrenched in every position they take. Up to this time there is no indication of any portion of Lee's army being detached for the defense of Richmond.

Official Records, Ser. I, Vol. 36, Part 2, 627.

It was by no accident that Lee beat Grant to Spotsylvania. On the morning of May 7th when rumors and reports indicated that Grant was preparing to retreat, General Gordon asked Lee "what he next expected from General Grant." Lee replied:

". . . General Grant is not going to retreat. He will move his army to Spotsylvania."

This notable prophecy of General Lee and its fulfilment by General Grant show that the brains of these two foemen had been working at the same problem. The known quantities in that problem were the aims of Grant to crush Lee and capture Richmond, to which had been added the results of the last two days' fighting. The unknown quantity which both were endeavoring to find was the next movement which the aggressor would probably make. Grant stood in his own place and calculated from his standpoint; Lee put himself in Grant's place and calculated from the same standpoint: and both found the same answer—Spotsylvania.

Having reached the same conclusion, both acted upon it with characteristic promptness; and then there was a race between them. Leaving their respective pioneer corps to bury the dead, and the surgeons and nurses to care for the wounded, they pressed toward the goal which their own convictions had set before them.

GORDON, *Reminiscences of the Civil War, pp. 269-270.*

Grant's decision to "fight it out on this line if it takes all summer," became one of the most quoted catch phrases of the Civil War, but if he had waited forty-eight hours, he probably would not have written the letter in which he made the statement.

On his subject General Gordon wrote:

Martin Luther once said: "Great soldiers make not many words, but when they speak the deed is done." General Grant measured up to Martin Luther's standard. He was a soldier of prompt and resolute action and of few words; but the few words he did speak in that letter to General Halleck would now seem to indicate that he overestimated the value of numbers and underestimated the steadfastness of the small army that opposed him. . . . The simple truth is, as General Grant afterward must have learned, there was no period of the war, since the day on which Lee assumed the command, when his army as a whole was less "shaky," more steadfast, more self-reliant, more devoted to its great leader and to the Southern cause. There was no period when that army more constantly exhibited "a spirit yet unquelled and high" than during the fearful experiences of 1864.

Fragments of broken iron are welded closest and strongest in the hottest fires. So the shattered corps of Lee's army seemed to be welded together by Grant's hammering—by the blood and the sweat and the fury of the flames that swept over and around them. In the tangled jungles of the Wilderness; through the incessant uproar by day and night at Spotsylvania; on the reddened banks of the North Anna; amidst the sickening slaughter of Cold Harbor,—everywhere, and on every field where the American armies met in deadly grapple, whether behind breastworks or in the open, whether assaulting or repelling, whether broken by the resistless impact or beating back with clubbed muskets the headlong charges of Grant,—these worn and battered soldiers of Lee seemed determined to compensate him for his paucity of numbers by a self-immolation and a steadfast valor never surpassed, if ever equalled.

I might safely rest the overwhelming vindication of these Southern soldiers against the statement of General Grant that they were "shaky" on the single and signal fact, that, from the Wilderness to Cold Harbor inclusive, in the brief space of twenty-eight days, they had placed *hors du [de] combat* about as many men as Lee commanded, killing, wounding, or capturing one of Grant's men for every Confederate in Lee's army. Or to state the fact in different form, had General Grant inflicted equal damage upon Lee's troops, the last Confederate of that army would have been killed, wounded, or captured, still leaving Grant with an army very much larger than any force that had been under Lee's command at any period of the campaign.

Wounded soldiers *escaping from the burning woods of the Wilderness, May 6, 1864.*

Federal gunners *race for position at Spotsylvania Court House, May 12, 1864.*

General Grant was not quite explicit as to what he meant by "this line." If he meant the overland route to Richmond which McDowell and Pope and Burnside and Hooker had each essayed and on which each had failed, as distinguished from the water route by the James River, which McClellan had attempted, General Grant found reasons to change his mind before the summer was ended. He did not "fight it out on this line"; for, long before the "all summer" limit which he had set was reached, the Union army found itself on an entirely different line—the James River or McClellan line. . . .

And the unbiased historian, in reviewing and analyzing the moves made by Grant on the vast chess-board reaching from the Wilderness to Petersburg, and the partial checkmates made by Lee in every game, will be forced to the conclusion that Lee's ubiquity must have been as great a marvel to Grant as Napoleon's was to the astounded Austrian [Bourrienne]. On May 5th Grant hurried his magnificent army, unmolested by even a picket shot, across the Rapidan to turn Lee's right; but the great leader of the Union forces found his wily antagonist not only checking him in the Wilderness, but on the next day (the 6th) turning the Union right flank and sweeping with the destructive energy of a whirlwind to the Union rear.

Protected from destruction by the density of the forest, Grant withdrew his bleeding army, and, under the cover of night, pressed with all possible speed to Spotsylvania; but there again he found Lee's vanguard across the line of his march, disputing his further advance. Again, after more than ten days of fighting and manoeuvring, of alternate successes and reverses, of desperate charges and deadly repulses, capturing breastworks only to see them recaptured, General Grant inaugurated the third and fourth and subsequent swiftly recurring movements, seeking by forced marches to plant his army in advantageous fields on Lee's right, only to find the Southern leader in possession of the coveted stronghold and successfully resisting all efforts to dislodge him. As Lee divined Grant's movement to Spotsylvania almost at the very instant the movement was taking shape in Grant's brain, so on each succeeding field he read the mind of the Union commander, and developed his own plans accordingly. There was no mental telepathy in all this. Lee's native and tutored genius enabled him to place himself in Grant's position, to reason out his antagonist's mental processes, to trace with accuracy the line of his marches, and to mark on the map the points of future conflict which were to become the blood-lettered mileposts marking Grant's compulsory halts and turnings in his zigzag route to Richmond. Finally at Cold Harbor, where a supreme effort was made to rip open Lee's lines by driving through them the stiff and compact Union columns, and where the slaughtered Federals presented the ghastliest scene ever witnessed on any field of the war, General Grant decided promptly and wisely to abandon further efforts on the north side and cross to the south side of the James River.

GORDON, *Reminiscences of the Civil War, pp. 292-298.*

In retrospect years later Grant said in his memoirs:

I have always regretted that the last assault at Cold Harbor was ever made. I might say the same thing of the assault of the 22nd of May, 1863, at Vicksburg. At Cold Harbor no advantage whatever was gained to compensate for the heavy loss we sustained. Indeed, the advantages other than those of relative losses, were on the Confederate side. Before that, the Army of Northern Virginia seemed to have acquired a wholesome regard for the courage, endurance, and soldierly qualities generally of the Army of the Potomac. They no longer wanted to fight them "one Confederate to five Yanks." Indeed, they seemed to have given up any idea of gaining any advantage of their antagonist in the open field. They had come to much prefer breastworks in their front to the Army of the Potomac. This charge seemed to revive their hopes temporarily; but it was of short duration. The effect upon the Army of the Potomac was the reverse. When we reached the James River, however, all effects of the battle of Cold Harbor seemed to have disappeared.

Grant was somewhat sensitive to criticism of his conduct of this campaign and in his memoirs he goes to some pains to show that the odds were not so greatly weighted in his favor. After explaining that there were differences in the methods used by the two armies in estimating the numbers of effective troops, he said also:

General Lee, who had led the Army of Northern Virginia in all these contests, was a very highly estimated man in the Confederate Army and States, and filled also a very high place in the estimation of the people and press of the Northern States. His praise was sounded throughout the entire North after every action he was engaged in: the number of his forces was always lowered and that of the National forces exaggerated. He was a large, austere man, and I judge difficult of approach to his subordinates. To be extolled by the entire press of the South after every engagement, and by a portion of the press for the North with equal vehemence, was calculated to give him the entire confidence of his troops and to make him feared by his antagonists. It was not an uncommon thing for my staff-officers to hear from Eastern officers, "Well, Grant has never met Bobby Lee yet." There were good and true officers who believe now that the Army of Northern Virginia was superior to the Army of the Potomac man to man. . . .

U. S. GRANT, *Personal Memoirs, Vol. II, pp. 276-277; 291-292.*

To Live or Die at Richmond

As month after month passed in that final year of the war the inevitable outcome of the one-sided struggle surely could be seen. Union forces growing ever stronger chopped the Southern Confederacy to fragments. The fall of Atlanta followed hard on the heels of Farragut's victory at Mobile Bay. Sherman devastated Georgia, captured Savannah, and turned northward through the Carolinas to join Grant. The capture of Wilmington closed the last Confederate port. "The condition of our army," said Gordon, "was daily becoming more desperate. Starvation, literal starvation, was doing its deadly work." Said General Long in his Memoirs:

. . . General Lee was fighting not alone against the army directly confronting him, but against all the military forces of the Northern States wherever situated. Grant's rank as commander-in-chief of the Federal armies enabled him to wield them all in concert for the great aim which he had in view, the defeat of Lee, and throughout the South armies were manoeuvring and marching for a single end, that of cutting at all points the strategic lines of the Confederacy, and so isolating the Army of Northern Virginia as to deprive it of all hope of assistance or reinforcement.

65

General Lee possessed no such comprehensive authority. He was commander of a single army only, and while his advice in relation to the movemnts of other armies was constantly asked by the Government, it was not always followed. The commander-in-chief was eventually given him, it is true, but too late for it to be more than an empty honor. Had he from the beginning of his contest with Grant possessed authoritative control of all the military resources of the Confederacy, the management of the war would certainly have been more efficient, and the armies of the Gulf States must have been handled with better judgment and success than they were under the orders of the civil authorities. The power of resistance of the Confederacy would probably have been protracted, and it is within the limits of possibility that eventual success in the effort to gain independence might have been attained, though at that late stage of the war this had become almost hopeless.

. . . If General Lee could at that time have taken the field and drawn Grant high up the country among the hills and mountain-spurs, whose friendly aid he knew so well how to apply, the Confederate power might have longer remained unbroken and honorable terms of peace have been obtained.

General Lee had actually taken steps to adopt a plan that offered the only hope of success, but this was overruled. The soundest advice in the land was disregarded, and it was decided that the Confederacy should live or die at Richmond. . . .

LONG, *Memoirs of Robert E. Lee, pp. 391-403.*

Front line operations *against Petersburg, 1864.*

Sharpshooters *in the trenches at Petersburg.*

One Thing Left to Do—Fight!

Confronted with overwhelming odds, want of men, want of subsistence, want of supplies and munitions, want of everything required for waging successful war, and with a line of defense becoming ever more tenuous, Lee saw clearly the possibility of being trapped by the combined armies of Grant and Sherman. There was an immediate need for action.

General John B. Gordon, whom Lee called into consultation, describes this portentous meeting:

During the first week in March, 1865, General Lee sent a messenger, about two o'clock in the morning, to summon me to his headquarters. It was one of the bitterest nights of that trying winter, and it required a ride of several miles to reach the house on the outskirts of Petersburg where the commanding-general made his headquarters. As I entered, General Lee, who was entirely alone, was standing at the fireplace, his arm on the mantel and his head resting on his arm as he gazed into the coal fire burning in the grate. He had evidently been up all the previous part of the night. For the first time in all my intercourse with him, I saw a look of painful depression on his face. Of course he had experienced many hours of depression, but he had concealed from those around him all evidence of discouragement. He had carried the burden in his own soul — wrapping his doubts and apprehensions in an exterior of cheerfulness and apparent confidence. The hour had come, however, when he could no longer carry alone the burden, or entirely conceal his forebodings of impending disaster. . . .

He opened the conference by directing me to read the reports of the different commands as he should hand them to me, and to carefully note every important fact contained in them.

The revelation was startling. Each report was bad enough, and all the distressing facts combined were sufficient, it seemed to me, to destroy all cohesive power and lead to the inevitable disintegration of any other army that was ever marshalled. . . .

The Tired Soldier.

When I had finished the inspection of this array of serious facts, and contemplated the bewildering woe which they presented, General Lee began his own analysis of the situation. He first considered the relative strength of his army and that of General Grant. The exact number of his own men was given in the reports before him—about 50,000, or 35,000 fit for duty. Against them he estimated that General Grant had in front of Richmond and Petersburg, or within his reach, about 150,000. Coming up from Knoxville was Thomas with an estimated force of 30,000 superb troops, to whose progress General Lee said we could offer practically no resistance—only a very small force of poorly equipped cavalry and detached bodies of infantry being available for that purpose.

"From the Valley," he said, "General Grant can and will bring upon us nearly 20,000, against whom I can oppose scarcely a vedette." This made an army of 200,000 well-fed, well-equipped men which General Grant could soon concentrate upon our force of 50,000, whose efficiency was greatly impaired by suffering. Sherman was approaching from North Carolina, and his force, when united with Schofield's, would reach 80,000. What force had we to confront that army? General Beauregard had telegraphed a few days before that, with the aid of Governor Vance's Home Guards, he could muster probably 20,000 to 25,000. But General Joseph E. Johnston had just sent a despatch saying in substance that General Beauregard had overestimated his strength, and that it would be nearer the truth to place the available Confederate force at from 13,000 to 15,000. So that the final summing up gave Grant the available crushing power of 280,000 men, while to resist this overwhelming force Lee had in round numbers by 65,000.

Having stated the facts, Lee then asked Gordon what it would be best to do under such conditions. Gordon replied:

General, it seems to me there are but three courses, and I name them in the order in which I think they should be tried:

First, make terms with the enemy, the best we can get.

Second, if that is not practicable, the best thing to do is to retreat—abandon Richmond and Petersburg, unite by rapid marches with General Johnston in North Carolina, and strike Sherman before Grant can join him; or,

Lastly, we must fight, and without delay.

Lee considered Gordon's statement and when he admitted he was in full agreement, Gordon suggested that the General should confer with President Davis or the Congress, or both combined, to find "the shortest way, consistent with honor, out of our troubles." The conference between the two generals broke up just after sunrise and Lee took the first train to Richmond where he spent two days. Promptly, on his return, he again summoned Gordon, who describes the result of Lee's visit to the Confederate capital:

He said nothing could be done at Richmond. The Congress did not seem to appreciate the situation. Of President Davis he spoke in terms of strong eulogy; of the strength of his convictions, of his devotedness, of his remarkable faith in the possibility of still winning our independence, and of his unconquerable will power. The nearest approach to complaint or criticism were the words which I can never forget: "You know that the President is very pertinacious in opinion and purpose." President Davis did not believe we could secure such terms as we could afford to accept.... Neither were the authorities ready to evacuate the capital and abandon our lines of defence, although every railroad except the South Side was already broken.

Having heard the commander's report of his interviews in Richmond, I asked:
"What, then, is to be done, general?"

He replied that there seemed to be but one thing that we could do—fight. To stand still was death. It could only be death if we fought and failed.

GORDON, *Reminiscences of the Civil War, pp. 385-394.*

Look Out Yank, We're Coming!

Driven by desperation to fight, Lee very quickly determined on a course of strategy. He would attempt to force Grant to shorten his lines by striking him in a vulnerable sector. Then, with a smaller front to protect, he would send a considerable part of his forces to the assistance of Johnston in North Carolina in the hope of defeating Sherman. If this plan succeeded, Johnston would then be in a position to combine with him against Grant.

The attack on the Union lines at Fort Stedman, which required elaborate preparation, was entrusted to Gordon and was planned for daybreak, March 25. Gordon recalls the breathless moment before this ill-fated battle:

All things ready, at 4 A.M., I stood on the top of the breastworks, with no one at my side except a single private soldier with rifle in hand, who was to fire the signal shot for the headlong rush. This night charge on the fort was to be across the intervening space covered with ditches, in one of which stood the watchful Federal pickets. There still remained near my works some of the débris of our obstructions, which had not been completely removed and which I feared might retard the rapid exit of my men; and I ordered it cleared away. The noise made by this removal, though slight, attracted the attention of a Union picket who stood on guard only a few rods from me, and he called out:

"What are you doing over there, Johnny? What is that noise? Answer quick or I'll shoot."

The pickets of the two armies were so close together at this point that there was an understanding between them, either expressed or implied, that they would not shoot each other down except when necessary. The call of this Union picket filled me with apprehension. I expected him to fire and start the entire picket-line to firing, thus giving the alarm to the fort, the capture of which depended largely upon the secrecy of my movement. The quick mother-wit of the private soldier at my side came to my relief. In an instant he replied:

"Never mind, Yank, Lie down and go to sleep. We are just gathering a little corn. You know rations are mighty short over here."

There was a narrow strip of corn which the bullets had not shot away still standing between the lines. The Union picket promptly answered: "All right, Johnny; go ahead and get your corn. I'll not shoot at you while you are drawing your rations."

Grant *breaks the Confederate Line at Petersburg, April 2, 1865.*

My troops stood in close column, ready for the hazardous rush upon Fort Stedman. While the fraternal dialogue in reference to drawing rations from the cornfield was progressing between the Union picket and the resourceful private at my side, the last of the obstructions in my front were removed, and I ordered the private to fire the signal for the assault. He pointed his rifle upward, with his finger on the trigger, but hesitated. His conscience seemed to get hold of him. He was going into the fearful charge, and he evidently did not feel disposed to go into eternity with the lie on his lips, although it might be a permissible war lie, by which he had thrown the Union picket off his guard. He evidently felt that it was hardly fair, to take advantage of the generosity and soldierly sympathy of his foe, who had so magnanimously assured him that he would not be shot while drawing his rations from the little field of corn. His hesitation surprised me, and I again ordered: "Fire your gun, sir." He at once called to his kind-hearted foe and said: "Hello, Yank, Wake up; we are going to shell the woods. Look out; we are coming." And with this effort to satisfy his conscience and even up accounts with the Yankee picket, he fired the shot and rushed forward in the darkness.

GORDON, *Reminiscences of the Civil War, pp. 407-410.*

The attack on Fort Stedman failed to accomplish its purpose and in withdrawing the Confederates suffered heavy losses. Grant now sent a flanking movement to the south and west of Petersburg and on April 1st won a smashing victory and again inflicted heavy losses on Lee's dwindling army. Next day the Federals broke through the Confederate lines southwest of Petersburg and forced Lee to retreat.

The Race Is Not to Them That's Got the Longest Legs to Run

April 2, 1865.

It was eleven o'clock of the morning when the despatch reached Richmond. It was the Sabbath-day. The city was at profound worship. The President was at St. Paul's Church. My wife was there (rest her spirit!) and heard the pastor, Mr. Minnegerode, read, *"The Lord is in his holy temple: let all the earth keep silence before him."* The full congregation rose, and the air whispered silence. The solemnity was broken as a swift despatch-bearer entered the portals and walked with quiet but rapid steps up the aisle to the chancel. He handed the President a sealed envelope. After reading, the President took his hat and walked with dignity down the aisle. Service was resumed, but presently came another messenger for some of the ladies, then another, and still another, and in a few moments the congregation, followed by the minister, giving up the sacred service, passed out and to their homes to prepare, in silent resignation, for whatever was to come.

LONGSTREET, *From Manassas to Appomattox, p. 607.*

Thus did Jefferson Davis learn that Richmond and Petersburg must be abandoned. That afternoon Lee ordered his troops to leave their lines everywhere and to rendezvous at Amelia Court House where he expected delivery of supplies and rations. This little village on the Richmond and Danville Railroad, was thirty-eight miles southwest of the Confederate capital and it was here that Lee hoped to concentrate his units and get them back in shape as a fighting organization. Through an unexplained error, however, there were no rations, and for six days the shattered remnants of the Army of Northern Virginia, stubbornly resisting, retreated before the relentless pressure of Grant's overwhelming forces.

Harried by hordes of cavalry the ragged columns pushed westward through country bare of food and sodden with rain. On the fifth night, worn and hungry, they were scattered out along the road to Appomattox.

Many of the men who had thrown away their arms and knapsacks were lying prone on the ground along the road-side, too much exhausted to march further, and only waiting for the enemy to come and pick them up as prisoners, while at short intervals there were wagons mired down, their teams of horses and mules lying in the mud, from which they struggled to extricate themselves until complete exhaustion had forced them to be still and wait for death to glaze their widely staring eyes, and still their quick gasping and panting for the breath which could scarcely reach some of them through the mud that almost closed their nostrils; but through all this a part of the army still trudged on, with their faith still strong, and only waiting for General Lee to say where they were to face about and fight. . . .

FRANK M. MYERS, *The Comanches: A History of White's Battalion, Virginia Cavalry, pp. 388-389.*

The Last of Ewell's Corps *April 6, 1865.*

The situation was desperate and while it was obvious to many of his officers that nothing could be gained by continuing the struggle, Lee hoped to extricate his army. At last on April 7 there began an exchange of notes between Grant and Lee which eventually brought the two leaders together to arrange the details of surrender. Charles Marshall, Lee's aide-de-camp and military secretary, describes the last bitter hours.

The march was continued during the 8th of April, with little interruption from the enemy, and in the evening we halted near Appomattox Court House, General Lee intending to march by way of Campbell Court House, through Pittsylvania County, toward Danville, with a view of opening communication with the Army of General Joseph E. Johnston, then retreating before General Sherman through North Carolina. General Lee's purpose was to unite with General Johnston to attack Sherman or call Johnston to his aid in resisting Grant, whichever might be found better. The exhausted troops were halted for rest on the evening of April 8 near Appomattox Court House, and the march was ordered to be resumed at 1 A.M. . . .

. . . General Lee and his staff turned out of the road into a dense wood to seek some rest. The general had a conference with some of the principal officers, at which it was determined to try to force our way the next morning with the troops of Gordon, supported by the cavalry under General Fitz Lee, the command of Longstreet bringing up the rear. . . .

When Lee closed his eyes on the eve of April 9th, he knew that the next day might bring surrender. He had agreed to meet General Grant between the picket lines of the two armies at 10 o'clock the following morning. Marshall bedded down with the other staff officers and those of General Longstreet and General Gordon. His narrative continues:

We lay upon the ground near the road, with our saddles for pillows, our horses picketed near by, eating the bark of trees for want of better provender, our faces covered with the capes of our overcoats to keep out the night air. Soon after one o'clock I was aroused by the sound of a column of infantry marching along the road. We were so completely surrounded by the swarming forces of General Grant that at first, when I awoke, I thought the passing column might be Federal soldiers.

I raised my head and listened intently. My doubts were quickly dispelled. I recalled the order to resume the march at that early hour, and knew that the troops I heard were moving forward to endeavor to force our way through the lines of the enemy at Appomattox Court House. I soon knew that the command that was passing consisted, in part at least, of Hood's old Texas brigade.

It was called the Texas brigade, although it was at times composed in part of regiments from other States. Sometimes there was a Mississippi regiment, sometimes an Arkansas regiment, and sometimes a Georgia regiment mingled with the Texans; but all the strangers called themselves Texans, and all fought like Texans.

On this occasion I recognized these troops, as they passed along the road in the dead of night, by hearing one of them repeat the Texan version of a passage of Scripture with which I was familiar—I mean with the Texan version. You will readily recall the original text when I repeat the Texan version of it that fell upon my ear as I lay in the woods by the roadside that dark night:

> The race is not to them that's got
> The longest legs to run,
> Nor the battel to that peopel
> That shoots the biggest gun.

This simple confession of faith assured me that the immortal brigade of Hood's Texans was marching to battle in the darkness.

Soon after they passed we were all astir, and our bivouac was at an end. We made our simple toilet, consisting mainly of putting on our caps and saddling our horses. We then proceeded to look for something to satisfy our now ravenous appetites.

Somebody had a little corn-meal, and somebody else had a tin can such as is used to hold hot water for shaving. A fire was kindled, and each man in his turn, according to rank and seniority, made a can of corn-meal gruel, and was allowed to keep the can until the gruel become cool enough to drink. General Lee, who reposed as we had done not far from us, did not, as far as I remember, have even such refreshment as I have described.

This was our last meal in the Confederacy. Our next was taken in the United States. . . .

As soon as we had all had our turn at the shaving-can, we rode toward Appomattox Court House. . . .

COL. CHARLES MARSHALL, *"The Last Days of Lee's Army."*
Century Magazine, Vol. 63, No. 6, (April, 1902), pp. 932-933.

I Would Rather Die a Thousand Deaths

April 9, 1865.

Colonel Venable of Lee's staff noted that:

At three o'clock on the morning of that fatal day General Lee rode forward, still hoping that he might break through the countless hordes of the enemy who hemmed us in. Halting a short distance in rear of our vanguard, he sent me on to General Gordon to ask him if he could break through the enemy. I found General Gordon and General Fitz Lee on their front line in the dim light of the morning arranging an attack. Gordon's reply to the message (I give the expressive phrase of the gallant Georgian) was this: "Tell General Lee I have fought my corps to a frazzle, and I fear I can do nothing unless I am heavily supported by Longstreet's corps."

When I bore this message back to General Lee he said, "Then there is nothing left me but to go and see General Grant, and I would rather die a thousand deaths."

LONG, *Memoirs of Robert E. Lee, p. 421.*

Longstreet records that:

Presently General Lee called to have me ride forward to him. He was dressed in a suit of new uniform, sword and sash, a handsomely embroidered belt, boots, and a pair of gold spurs. At first approach his compact figure appeared as a man in the flush vigor of forty summers, but as I drew near, the handsome apparel and brave bearing failed to conceal his profound depression. He stood near the embers of some burned rails, received me with graceful salutation, and spoke at once of affairs in front and the loss of his subsistence stores. He remarked that the advanced columns stood against a very formidable force, which he could not break through, while General Meade was at my rear ready to call for all the work that the rear-guard could do, and, closing with the expression that it was not possible for him to get along, requested my view. I asked if the bloody sacrifice of his army could in any way help the cause in other quarters. He thought not. Then, I said, your situation speaks for itself.

LONGSTREET, *From Manassas to Appomattox, pp. 624-625.*

Said General E. P. Alexander, chief of artillery of the First Corps:

Soon after sunrise, on the morning of the 9th, I came up with General Lee, halted, with his staff, by the roadside, a mile and a half from the village. Gordon, who was in advance, was already engaged, and the increasing sound of cannon and musketry told that the enemy was in heavy force.

The progress of the column was stopped, and trains were parked in the fields, while guns and infantry moved forward to the sound of firing. General Lee called me to him, and, walking off from the group, sat down on a log and said: "The enemy seems to be across our road in force this morning. What have we got to do?"

Now, our artillery had not been seriously engaged during the retreat, and was never in better humor for a fight. The cannoneers, for some days before, beginning, perhaps, to appreciate the situation, had called out along the road, "Don't let us surrender any of this ammunition! We have been saving ammunition all the war! We did not save it to be surrendered."

I told General Lee of this, and said that I could show up near forty guns with one hundred rounds apiece, if he wished to give battle. He replied that the force in front of us was too great, that while he had, perhaps, fifteen thousand infantry, half of them were mere fragments of different commands, unorganized and largely without arms or ammunition, and that he could scarcely concentrate an effective force of eight thousand men, which was too small to accomplish any valuable results. I was not unprepared to hear this decision, for the last forty-eight hours had made apparent the desperate condition to which we were reduced, and I had views on the matter, which I was glad of so favorable an opportunity to express. So I spoke up:

"Then, general, we have choice of but two courses: to surrender, or to order the army to disperse, and, every man for himself, to take to the woods and make his way either to Johnston's army in Carolina, or to his home, taking his arms, and reporting to the governor of his State. And of these alternatives the latter is the best . . . spare us the mortification of your asking Grant for terms, and being told, 'Unconditional surrender.' Save us from that!"

General Lee listened to me quietly until I had quite finished, and then he said:

"Suppose I were to adopt your suggestion, how many do you suppose would get away?"

I replied: "I think two thirds of us could get away. We should be like rabbits and partridges in the bushes, and they could not scatter like that to catch us."

"Well," he said, "I have less than sixteen thousand infantry with arms in their hands. Even if two thirds of these got away it would be too small a force to accomplish any useful result, either with Johnston or with the governors of the States. But few would go to Johnston, for their homes have been overrun by the enemy, and the men will want to go first and look after their families. As to any help from Europe, I have never believed in it. I appreciate that the surrender of this army is, indeed, the end of the Confederacy. But that result is now inevitable, and must be faced. And, as Christian men, we have no right to choose a course from pride or personal feelings. We have simply to see what we can do best for our country and people. Now, if I should adopt your suggestions and order this army to disperse, the men, going homeward, would be under no control, and, moreover, would be without food. They are already demoralized by four years of war, and would supply their wants by violence and plunder. They would soon become little better than bands of robbers. A state of society would result, through the South, from which it would require years to recover. The enemy's cavalry, too, would pursue to catch at least the general officers, and would harass and devastate sections that otherwise they will never visit. Moreover," he said, "as to myself, I am too old to go bushwhacking, and even if it were right to order the army to disperse, the only course for me to pursue would be to surrender myself to General Grant. But," he added, "I can tell you for your comfort that Grant will not demand an 'unconditional surrender.' He will give us honorable and liberal terms, simply requiring us not to take up arms again until exchanged. . . ."

BRIG. GEN. E. P. ALEXANDER, *"Lee at Appomatox, Personal Recollections of the Break-up of the Confederacy." Century Magazine, Vol. 63, No. 6 (April, 1902), pp. 925-927.*

Soon after this conversation with Alexander, Lee's Adjutant, Colonel Taylor, joined him. Taylor had been occupied the previous night with parking the trains.

After making my report the general said to me, "Well, colonel, what are we to do?"

In reply a fear was expressed that it would be necessary to abandon the trains, which had already occasioned us such great embarrassment; and the hope was indulged that, relieved of this burden, the army could make good its escape.

"Yes," said the general, "perhaps we could; but I have had a conference with these gentlemen around me, and they agree that the time has come for capitulation."

"Well, sir," I said, "I can only speak for myself; to me any other fate is preferable—"

"Such is my individual way of thinking," interrupted the general.

"But," I immediately added, "of course, general, it is different with you. You have to think of these brave men and decide not only for yourself, but for them."

"Yes," he replied; "it would be useless and therefore cruel to provoke the further effusion of blood, and I have arranged to meet General Grant with a view to surrender, and wish you to accompany me."

I shrank from this interview, and while I could not then, and cannot now, justfy my conduct, I . . . did not accompany my chief in this trying ordeal.

WALTER H. TAYLOR, *Four Years with General Lee, pp. 151-153.*

Ninth of April

The meeting between Grant and Lee was held in the parlor of the home of Major Wilmer McLean, who, by chance, had owned the farm on Bull Run where, in the first battle of that name, the initial clash had occurred. Lee arrived first, in company with his aide-de-camp, Colonel Charles Marshall, and Colonel Orville E. Babcock of Grant's staff. Colonel Marshall was the only southern witness of the surrender. Said Col. Marshall:

General Lee, Colonel Babcock, and I sat in the parlor for about half an hour, when a large party of mounted men arrived, and in a few minutes General Grant came into the room, accompanied by his staff and a number of Federal officers of rank, among whom were General Ord and General Sheridan.

General Grant greeted General Lee very civilly, and they engaged in conversation for a short time about their former acquaintance during the Mexican War.

Some other Federal officers took part in the conversation, which was terminated by General Lee saying to General Grant that he had come to discuss the terms of surrender of his army, as indicated in his note of that morning, and he suggested to General Grant to reduce his proposition to writing. General Grant assented, and Colonel Ely S. Parker of his staff moved a small table from the opposite side of the room, and placed it by General Grant, who sat facing, General Lee.

When General Grant had written his letter in pencil, he took it to General Lee, who remained seated. General Lee read the letter, and called General Grant's attention to the fact that he required the surrender of the horses of the cavalry as if they were public horses. He told General Grant that Confederate cavalrymen owned their horses, and that they would need them for planting a spring crop. General Grant at once accepted the suggestion, and interlined the provision, allowing the retention by the men of the horses that belonged to them.

The terms of the letter having been agreed to, General Grant directed Colonel Parker to make a copy of it in ink, and General Lee directed me to write his acceptance.

Colonel Parker took the light table upon which General Grant had been writing to the opposite corner of the room, and I accompanied him. There was an inkstand in the room, but the ink was so thick that it was of no use. I had a small boxwood inkstand which I always carried, and I gave it, with my pen, to Colonel Parker, who proceeded to copy General Grant's letter.

While he was so engaged I sat near the end of the sofa on which General Sheridan was sitting, and we entered into conversation. In the midst of it General Grant, who sat nearly diagonally across the room and was talking with General Lee, turned to General Sheridan and said:

"General Sheridan, General Lee tells me that he has some twelve hundred of our people prisoners, who are sharing with his men, and that none of them have anything to eat. How many rations can you spare?"

General Sheridan replied: "About twenty-five thousand."

General Grant turned to General Lee and said: "General, will that be enough?"

General Lee replied: "More than enough."

Thereupon General Grant said to General Sheridan: "Direct your commissary to send twenty-five thousand rations to General Lee's commissary."

General Sheridan at once sent an officer to give the necessary orders.

When Colonel Parker had concluded the copying of General Grant's letter, I sat down at the same table and wrote General Lee's answer.

General Lee *leaving the McLean House after the surrender, April 9, 1865.*

When General Grant had signed the copy of his letter made by Colonel Parker, and General Lee had signed the answer, Colonel Parker handed to me General Grant's letter and I handed to him General Lee's reply, and the work was done. Some further conversation of a general nature took place, in the course of which General Grant said to General Lee that he had come to the meeting as he was and without his sword, because he did not wish to detain General Lee until he could send back to his wagons, which were several miles away. This was the only reference made by anyone to the subject of dress on that occasion.

General Lee had prepared himself for the meeting with more than usual care, and was in full uniform, wearing a very handsome sword and sash. This was doubtless the reason for General Grant's reference to himself.

At last General Lee took leave of General Grant, saying that he would return to his headquarters and designate the officers who were to act on our side in arranging the details of the surrender. We mounted our horses, which the orderly was holding in the yard, and rode away, a number of Federal officers standing on the porch in front of the house, looking at us.

COL. CHARLES MARSHALL, *"The Last Days of Lee's Army."*
Century Magazine, Vol. 63, No. 6 (April, 1902), pp. 934-935.

Great as the ordeal of arranging terms of surrender with Grant must have been, Lee had now to face the even more bitter duty of telling his own men what he had done. Alexander describes the scene as Lee approached the Confederate lines.

I think it was after three o'clock when we saw Lee returning. We wished to express to him in some way our sympathy and affection, and I ordered all the cannoneers to be brought from the guns and formed in line along the road, with instructions to uncover in silence as he rode by. He had hardly reached the line, however, when some one started a cheer, which was taken up by others, and then both infantry and artillery broke their line and crowded about his horse in the road. The general stopped and made a short address. Briefly, it was about as follows:

"I have done for you all that it was in my power to do. You have done all your duty. Leave the result to God. Go to your homes and resume your occupations. Obey the laws and become good citizens as you were soldiers."

There was not a dry eye in the crowd that heard him, and even he seemed deeply moved. The men crowded around to try and shake his hand or touch his horse, and some appealed to him to get us all exchanged and try it again; but he made no reply to such remarks. Then he rode on to his camp, and the crowd broke up, and then ranks were formed once more and marched off to bivouac, and the Army of Northern Virginia was an army no longer, but a lot of captives awaiting their paroles. But it had written its name in history, and no man need be ashamed of its record, though its last chapter is a story of disaster. And surely those qualities in its commander for which men are loved and admired by friend and foe shone out here with no less luster than on any other field.

BRIG. GEN. E. P. ALEXANDER, *"Lee at Appomattox, Personal Recollections of the Break-up of the Confederacy." Century Magazine, Vol. 63, No. 6 (April, 1902), p. 930.*

An Affectionate Farewell

There was no final review, no speech making, no theatrics. Grant and Lee met again on April 10 between the lines and had a friendly talk which lasted about an hour, and during the day General Meade and other Union leaders sought him out. General Lee published his last order, reported the surrender to President Davis, and on April 12, the surrender having been com-

pleted, he quietly broke camp and started home. With him rode Taylor, Marshall, and Cooke, and for some distance along the way, despite his protest, he was accompanied by a handsomely mounted honor escort of twenty-five Union cavalrymen.

Hd. qrs. Army of N. Va.
April 10, 1865.

General Orders
No. 9

After four years of arduous service marked by unsurpassed courage and fortitude, the Army of Northern Virginia has been compelled to yield to overwhelming numbers and resources.

I need not tell the brave survivors of so many hard fought battles, who have remained steadfast to the last, that I have consented to this result from no distrust of them; but feeling that valor and devotion could accomplish nothing that could compensate for the loss that must have attended the continuance of the contest, I determined to avoid the useless sacrifice of those whose past services have endeared them to their countrymen.

By the terms of the agreement, officers and men can return to their homes and remain until exchanged. You will take with you the satisfaction that proceeds from the consciousness of duty faithfully performed; and I earnestly pray that a Merciful God will extend to you His blessing and protection.

With an unceasing admiration of your constancy and devotion to your Country, and and a grateful remembrance of your kind and generous consideration for myself, I bid you all an affectionate farewell.

(Sgd) R. E. Lee
Genl.

From General Lee's Letter Book. Quoted by D. S. FREEMAN, in
R. E. Lee, A Biography, Vol. IV, pp. 154-155.

Rebs *taking the oath at Richmond, 1865.*

The man who returned from Appomattox. *From a photograph by Mathew Brady, April 1865, in the Collections of the Library of Congress.*

V. I BELIEVE IT TO BE THE DUTY OF EVERYONE TO UNITE IN THE RESTORATION OF THE COUNTRY

As Lee had led in battle, he now continued to lead in peace. "Go home," he counselled, "all you boys who fought with me, and help to build up the shattered fortunes of our old state." To Josiah Tattnall, distinguished naval officer at Savannah, Georgia, he wrote:

Like yourself, I have, since the cessation of hostilities, advised all with whom I have conversed on the subject, who come within the terms of the President's proclamations, to take the oath of allegiance, and accept in good faith the amnesty offered. But I have gone further, and have recommended to those who were excluded from their benefits, to make application under the *proviso* of the proclamation of the 29th of May, to be embraced in its provisions. Both classes, in order to be restored to their former rights and privileges, were required to perform a certain act, and I do not see that an acknowledgment of fault is expressed in one more than the other. The war being at an end, the Southern States having laid down their arms, and the questions at issue between them and the Northern States having been decided, I believe it to be the duty of every one to unite in the restoration of the country, and the reestablishment of peace and harmony. . . .

R. E. LEE TO CAPTAIN JOSIAH TATTNALL, *Sept. 7, 1865.* IN JONES

Personal Reminiscences of General Robert E. Lee, p. 205.

On discovering that he was among those excluded from the provisions of amnesty contained in the President's proclamation Lee applied for a pardon.

Richmond, Va., June 13, 1865.

Lieut.-Gen. U. S. GRANT, *Commanding the Armies of the United States:*

GENERAL: Upon reading the President's proclamation of the 29th ultimo, I came to Richmond to ascertain what was proper or required of me to do, when I learned that with others I was to be indicted for treason by the grand jury at Norfolk. I had supposed that the officers and men of the Army of Northern Virginia were, by the terms of their surrender, protected by the United States Government from molestation so long as they conformed to its conditions. I am ready to meet any charges that may be preferred against me. I do not wish to avoid trial, but if I am correct as to the protection granted by my parole, and am not to be prosecuted, I desire to comply with the provisions of the President's proclamation, and therefore inclose the required application, which I request in that event may be acted on.

I am, with great respect, your obedient servant,

R. E. LEE

Official Records, Ser. I, Vol .46, Part 3, pp. 1275-1276.

Richmond, Va., June 13, 1865.

His Excellency ANDREW JOHNSON, President of the United States.

SIR: Being excluded from the provisions of the amnesty and pardon contained in the proclamation of the 29th ult., I hereby apply for the benefits and full restoration of all rights and privileges extended to those included in its terms. I graduated at the Military Academy at West Point in June, 1829; resigned from the United States Army, April, 1861; was a general in the Confederate Army, and included in the surrender of the Army of Northern Virginia, April 9, 1865. I have the honour to be, very respectfully,

Your obedient servant
R. E. LEE

R. E. LEE [JR.], *Recollections and letters, pp. 164-165.*

Grant endorsed Lee's application and forwarded it to President Johnson. At the same time he supported Lee's view that paroled prisoners of war could not be tried for treason so long as they observed their paroles. He asked that all indictments found against paroled prisoners of war be quashed. No action was taken on Grant's recommendation, but Lee was never arrested, and after the general amnesty proclamation of December 25, 1868, the indictments against him and other general officers of the Confederacy were nolle prossed. *By the adoption of the Fourteenth Amendment, however, Lee was forever barred from holding state or Federal office.*

States Rights and the Constitution

In December, 1866, Lee wrote a careful analysis of his views on the constitutionl issues in-volved in secession and on the long range political outlook. This analysis was prepared at the request of the British historian, Sir John Dalberg Acton, later Lord Acton, who was particu-larly anxious to gain the Southern point of view. This letter is important as it gives Lee full expression on a subject on which he was wont to be silent.

Lexington, Vir., 15 Dec., 1866.

Sir,—Although your letter of the 4th ulto. has been before me some days un-answered, I hope you will not attribute it to a want of interest in the subject, but to my in-ability to keep pace with my correspondence. As a citizen of the South I feel deeply indebted to you for the sympathy you have evinced in its cause, and am conscious that I owe your kind consideration of myself to my connection with it. The influence of current opinion in Europe upon the current politics of America must always be salutary; and the importance of the questions now at issue in the United States, involving not only constitutional free-dom and constitutional government in this country, but the progress of universal liberty and civilization, invests your proposition with peculiar value, and will add to the obligation which every true American must owe you for your efforts to guide that opinion aright. Amid the conflicting statements and sentiments in both countries, it will be no easy task to discover the truth, or to relieve it from the mass of prejudice and passion, with which it has been covered by party spirit. I am conscious of the compliment conveyed in your request for my opinion as to the light in which American politics should be viewed, and had I the ability, I have not the time to enter upon a discussion, which was commenced by the founders of the constitution and has been continued to the present day. I can only say that while I have considered the preservation of the constitutional power of the General Government to be the foundation of our peace and safety at home and abroad, I yet believe that the maintenance of the rights and authority reserved to the states and to the people, not only essential to the adjustment and balance of the general system, but the safeguard to the con-tinuance of a free government. I consider it as the chief source of stability to our political system, whereas the consolidation of the states into one vast republic, sure to be aggressive abroad and despotic at home, will be the certain precursor of that ruin which has over-whelmed all those that have preceded it. I need not refer one so well acquainted as you are with American history, to the State papers of Washington and Jefferson, the representatives of the federal and democratic parties, denouncing consolidation and centralization of power, as tending to the subversion of State Governments, and to despotism. The New England States, whose citizens are the fiercest opponents of the Southern states, did not always avow the opinions they now advocate. Upon the purchase of Louisiana by Mr. Jefferson, they virtually asserted the right of secession through their prominent men; and in the con-vention which assembled at Hartford in 1814, they threatened the disruption of the Union unless the war should be discontinued. The assertion of this right has been repeatedly made by their politicians when their party was weak, and Massachusetts, the leading state in hositlity to the South, declares in the preamble to her constitution, that the people of that commonwealth "have the sole and exclusive right of governing themselves as a free sovereign and independent state, and do, and forever hereafter shall, exercise and enjoy every power, jurisdiction, and right which is not, or may hereafter be by them expressly delegated to the United States of America in congress assembled." Such has been in sub-stance the language of other State governments, and such the doctrine advocated by the leading men of the country for the last seventy years. Judge Chase, the present Chief Justice of the U.S., as late as 1850, is reported to have stated in the Senate, of which he was a member, that he "knew of no remedy in case of the refusal of a state to perform its stipulations," thereby acknowledging the sovereignty and independence of state action. But I will not weary you with this unprofitable discussion. Unprofitable because the judgment of reason has been displaced by the arbitrament of war, waged for the purpose as avowed of maintaining the union of the states. If, therefore, the result of the war is to be considered as having decided that the union of the states is inviolable and perpetual under the constitution, it naturally follows that it is as incompetent for the general government to impair its integrity by the exclusion of a state, as for the states to do so by secession; and that the existence and rights of a state by the constitution are as indestructible as the union itself. The legitimate consequence then must be the perfect equality of rights of all the states; the exclusive right of each to regulate its internal affairs under rules established by the constitution, and the right of each state to prescribe for itself the qualifications of suffrage. The South has contended only for the supremacy of the constitution, and the just administration of the laws made in pursuance of it. Virginia to the last made great efforts to save the Union, and urged harmony and compromise. Senator Douglass, [Douglas], in his remarks upon the compromise bill recommended by the committee of thirteen in 1861, stated that every member from the South, including Messrs. Toombs and Davis, expressed their willingness to accept the proposition of Senator Crittendon from Kentucky, as a final settlement of the controversy, if sustained by the republican party, and that the only difficulty in the way of an amicable adjustment was with the republican party. Who then is responsible for the war? Although the South would have preferred any honorable compromise to the fratricidal war which has taken place, she now accepts in good faith its constitutional results, and receives without reserve the amendment which has already been made to the constitution for the extinction of slavery. That is an event that has been long sought, though in a different way, and by none has it been more earnestly desired than by citizens of Virginia. In other respects I trust that the constitution may undergo no change, but that it may be handed down to succeeding generations in the form we received it from our forefathers. The desire I feel that the Southern states should possess the good opinion of one whom I esteem as highly as yourself, has caused me to extend my remarks farther than I intended, and I fear it has led me to exhaust your patience. If what I have said should serve to give any information as regards American politics, and enable you to enlighten public opinion as to the true interests of this distracted country, I hope you will pardon its prolixity.

RILEY, *General Robert E. Lee After Appomattox, pp. 237-241.*

President Lee of Washington College

How Robert E. Lee became a college president is told by Professor Alexander L. Nelson, a member of General Lee's faculty. This sketch was first printed in the "Lee Memorial Number," January, 1907, of the Wake Forest Student, a magazine published by Wake Forest College. It was reprinted in 1922 in a memorial volume, General Robert E. Lee After Appomattox, edited by Franklin L. Riley, Professor of History, Washington and Lee University.

When the war closed Washington College was a wreck, but the board of trustees, animated by indomitable Scotch-Irish pluck, determined to resuscitate it. It was announced that the board would meet on the 4th day of August, 1865. The members of the faculty were present by invitation, as most interested spectators.

Several highly respectable gentlemen and scholars were placed in nomination for president and their merits discussed.

Just then Col. Bolivar Christian arose and said, in a somewhat hesitating manner, that he deemed it his duty to make a statement, before the vote was taken, which might have some influence on the election. He then said that a lady friend of his, who was also a friend of Miss Mary Lee, daughter of General Robert E. Lee, recently told him that Miss Mary Lee had remarked to her that while the Southern people were willing and ready to give her father everything that he might need, no offer had ever been made him by which he could earn a living for himself and family.

A member asked Colonel Christian if he nominated General Lee. No, he replied, he would not do that, but he merely wanted the board to know what Miss Mary Lee had said.

Then various members of the board said what a great thing it would be for the college if the services of General Lee could be secured, and wondered if there was any chance of doing so.

At length, after repeated urging, Colonel Christian did make the nomination. All other names were immediately withdrawn and the roll was called, and General Lee was unanimously elected.

Then there was a pause, and silence prevailed for some moments. The board seemed oppressed with the gravity of the situation, and seemed to feel that they had acted rashly. How could they announce to the world that they had elected to the presidency of a broken-down college not only the greatest man in the South, but in many respects the greatest man in the world? And yet it was only brave men who could seize an opportunity like this. "There is a tide in the affairs of men which, taken at its flood, leads on to fortune."

At length a member summoned courage to say that having taken that step, they must go forward, and he moved that a committee of five members, with the rector, be appointed to draft a letter to General Lee apprising him of his election and urging his acceptance. Another member suggested that it would not avail to send a letter through the mail, but that it must be conveyed and presented by a personal representative, and that there was no one so well qualified for that mission as the rector.

Judge Brockenbrough, the rector, was a large man of imposing appearance, of courtly manners, a good talker and an eloquent speaker. He had been federal judge of the western district of Virginia, and had for many years conducted a flourishing law school in Lexington.

The judge arose at once and, thanking the member for his kind words, said that he could not go; and glancing down at his well-worn clothes, said he could not make an appearance in General Lee's presence dressed as he was, and that those were the best clothes he had, and that he had no money whatever to buy others.

Mr. Hugh Barclay, a member of the board, who also was a large man, replied that one of his sons who lived in the North had sent him a suit of broadcloth which he thought would fit Judge Brockenbrough pretty well and that if he would wear this suit he would be welcome to it. The judge thanked him, but said there was still another difficulty. It would be quite a journey to Powhatan county, where General Lee was residing, and would necessitate some expense, and he had no money and the college had none.

Colonel McLaughlin, another trustee, who was ever alive to the interests of the college, and who knew everthing that occurred in town, said there was a lady living in Lexington who owned a farm in Buckingham country and who had recently secured the money for a crop of tobacco, and that the college could borrow some of it.

Judge Brockenbrough, thus equipped and supplied, went on his mission. When he returned he reported that General Lee was willing to take the matter under consideration.

On the 24th of August General Lee wrote that he would accept the office of President of Washington College under certain conditions, one of which was that he could not undertake to give instruction in classes, but could only undertake general supervision. The conditions imposed were readily accepted by the board and the announcement of General Lee's acceptance was made public.

Money was borrowed and every effort made to place the college in working order. On the 18th of September, 1865, General Lee rode into town on "Traveller."

RILEY, *After Appomattox*, pp. 1-4.

The inauguration of General Lee, as President of Washington College, October 2, 1865, was reported to the New York Herald by a staff correspondent and the story was republished in the Lexington Gazette of October 11, 1865.

General Robert E. Lee was to-day installed president of Washington College. There was no pomp of parade. The exercises of installation were the simplest possible—an exact and barren compliance with the required formula of taking the oath by the new President, and nothing more—was in accordance with the special request of General Lee. . . .

The installation took place at 9 A.M. in a recitation room of the college. In this room were seated the faculty and students, the ministers of the town churches, a magistrate and the county clerk, the last two officials being necessary to the ceremonial. General Lee was inducted into the room by the board of trustees. At his entrance and introduction all in the room arose, bowed and then became seated. Prayer by Rev. Dr. White, pastor of the Presbyterian church, directly followed. To me it was a noticeable fact, and perhaps worthy of record, that he prayed for the President of the United States. Altogether it was a most fitting and impressive prayer.

The prayer ended, Judge Brockenbrough, chairman of the board of trustees, stated the object of their coming together, to install General Lee as President of Washington College. He felt the serious dignity of the occasion, but it was a seriousness and a dignity that should be mingled with heartfelt joy and gladness. Passing a brief eulogy upon General Lee, and congratulating the board and the college and its present and future students, on having obtained one so loved and great and worthy to preside over the college, he said he could say more had it not been voted against speechmaking. During the delivery of these few words—and they came, despite the prohibitory voting, very near culminating to the dignity of a set as well as eloquent speech, General Lee remained standing, his arms quietly folded and calmly and steadfastly looking into the eyes of the speaker. Justice William White, at the instance of Judge Brockenbrough, now administered the oath of office to General Lee. For the benefit of those curious to know the nature of this new oath to which General Lee has just subscribed, and as it is brief, I give it entire. It is as follows:

"I do swear that I will, to the best of my skill and judgment, faithfully and truly discharge the duties required of me by an act entitled, 'An Act for incorporating the rector and trustees of Liberty Hall Academy,' without favor, affection or partiality. So help me God."

General Lee was dressed in a plain but elegant suit of gray. His appearance indicated the enjoyment of good health—better, I should say, than when he surrendered his army at Appomattox Court House, the first and only occasion before the present of my having seen him. . . .

RILEY, *After Appomattox*, pp. 12-15.

Professor Edward S. Joynes, who held the chair of Modern Languages at Washington College while General Lee was president, gives an appraisal of Lee as college president in an article which first appeared in the Richmond, Va., Dispatch, January 27, 1901. This was later reprinted in the Southern Historical Society Papers, XXVIII, 243-246.

My recollections shall be chiefly of General Lee as college president. It is as such that he is chiefly present to my memory—always for admiration, sometimes for contrast with later experiences. I will not enlarge upon the quiet dignity and patience with which he always presided over our often wordy and tedious meetings, his perfect impartiality, and unwearied courtesy, his manifest effort to sink his own personality, as if to minimize the influence which he knew attached to his own views, and to leave to the faculty as a body, and to each member of it, the fullest sense of authority and independence.

Indeed, nowhere else in all my wide experience have I found so much of personal dignity and influence attached to the professorship as at Lexington; and this was largely due to the courtesy and deference with which General Lee treated the faculty, and every member of it, in both official and private relations. Yet none the less, on those rare occasions when it became necessary, did he assert the full measure of his authority. He rarely spoke in faculty meetings, and then only at the close of debate—usually to restate the question at issue, seldom with any decided expression of his own opinion or wish.

I remember on one occasion a professor quoted a certain regulation in the by-laws. Another replied that it had become a dead letter. "Then," said General Lee, "let it be repealed. A dead letter inspires disrespect for the whole body of laws."

When General Lee became President of Washington College it had been required that students should occupy the college dormitories; only a few of the older students were permitted to lodge in town. General Lee reversed this rule. As a measure of discipline it was required that all students board and lodge in the families of the town; to lodge in the dormitories was accorded as a privilege. He said the young boys needed the influence of family life; the dormitories he regarded as offering temptations to license. The result vindicated the wisdom of his view.

In dealing with the young men General Lee had a truly marvelous success. The students fairly worshipped him, and deeply dreaded his displeasure; yet so kind, affable, and gentle was he toward them that all loved to approach him. Still, an official summons to his office struck terror even into the most hardened.

A young fellow, whose general record was none too good, was summoned to answer for absence. He stated his excuse, and then, hesitatingly, he added another and another. "Stop Mr. . . . . . .," said General Lee, "one good reason should be sufficient to satisfy an honest mind," with emphasis on the word "honest" that spoke volumes.

Another, an excellent student, now a distinguished lawyer in Tennessee, was once beguiled into an unexcused absence. The dreaded summons came. With his heart in his boots he entered General Lee's office. The General met him smiling: "Mr. M., I am glad to see you are better." "But General, I have not been sick." "Then I am glad to see you have better news from home." "But General, I have had no bad news." "Ah," said the General, "I took it for granted that nothing less than sickness or distressing news from home could have kept you from your duty." Mr. M. told me, in relating the incident, that he then felt as if he wished the earth would open and swallow him.

To a recalcitrant student, who was contending for what he thought his rights as a man, I once heard General Lee say: "Obedience to lawful authority is the foundation of manly character," — in those very words.

On rare occasions of disorder, actual or threatened, General Lee would post a manuscript address to students on the bulletin board. These were known among the boys as his "General Orders." They never failed of their effect. No student would have dared to violate General Lee's expressed wish or appeal—if he had done so the students themselves would have driven him from the college.

I wish to add one other important fact, illustrating General Lee's view of discipline, in a case of frequent occurrence. He held idleness to be not negative, but a positive vice. It often happened that the plea was made that an idle student was doing no harm and indirectly deriving benefits, etc., General Lee said, "No, a young man is always doing something; if not good then harm to himself and others." So that merely persistent idleness was with him always sufficient cause for dismissal.

General Lee's ideal of education was the training of manly character, and that, for him, meant Christian character. To a venerable minister of Lexington he said: " I shall be disappointed, sir—I shall fail in the leading object that brought me here—unless these young men all become consistent Christians." When he came to Lexington the old president's house was in a sadly dilapidated condition. The Trustees desired to build at once a suitable home for the president's residence. But General Lee insisted that the first money collected should be devoted to building a chapel, and he would not allow the president's house to be begun until the chapel had been completed and furnished—that chapel beneath which now rests his own beautiful mausoleum. Here daily religious services were held at an early hour by the ministers of Lexington in rotation—but not on Sunday, for General Lee preferred that the students should go to the church of their parents in the town.

General Lee had very well defined opinions on educational subjects. In quoting some of these it might, perhaps, be unjust to apply them to present conditions, which, of course, could not then be foreseen. He was a strong advocate of practical, even technical education, as was shown by his plans for Washington College; but he was equally firm in his support of training studies and liberal culture. I have often heard him say it had been his lifelong regret that he had not completed his classical education (in which, however, he had a respectable scholarship) before going to West Point. Also, he did not believe in separate technical schools, but thought "that scientific and professional studies could best be taught when surrounded by the liberalizing influence of a literary institution." Hence, he sought to unite all these in the development of Washington College.

Especially, General Lee did not believe in a military education for others than army officers. Military education, he used to say, is an unfortunate necessity for the soldier, but the worst possible preparation for civil life. "For many years," he said, "I have observed the failure in business pursuits of men who have resigned from the army. It is very rare that any one of them has achieved success."

RILEY, *After Appomattox, pp. 16-21.*

Next Time Use Less Powder

The following incident described by J. W. Ewing of Rome, Georgia, reveals the subtle relationship which developed between Lee and the students of Washington College.

After the term opened and winter had set in, Graham, Allison, Cockrill and I rented a private room in the college buildings where we could study and keep warm between recitations. We would each in turn buy a load of wood, as needed. This was sawed into stove lengths and piled up in the corner of the room. The winter was a bitter one, with snow on the ground for eleven weeks successively. It had been Graham's turn to buy a cord of hickory. This was disappearing faster than ever. So fast, in fact, that all realized our stove was not the only one that was being fed. The college wood pile was nearly 200 feet from the building and the janitor lazy, and Graham had his suspicion. He selected a round hickory stick, bored into it with a big auger, filled the hole with powder and sealed it with clay. This was put back on the wood pile by Graham, who warned us under no circumstances to put that particular stick in our stove. The next morning early there was a tremendous explosion in the room of the professor of modern languages, Dr. Edward S. Joynes. His stove was blown to pieces and the college building set on fire. Of course, it created something of a sensation.

Before the services in chapel, General Lee prefaced his remarks with the statement that the faculty had promulgated no rules for student government, that each and every one was presumed to be a gentleman and that by tacit agreement the control of the students was left to the student body and the individual sense of honor of each student. He then said he would be glad to have any one who knew about the explosion call at his office during the forenoon. Graham knew, or felt, that it was his "depth charge" that had done the work, so at his request, about 11 A.M. he and I together went to the General's office.

Lord Wolseley, the commander of the English armies, was in Lexington, where he had come to pay his respects to our General. Seeing that the General was engaged, we were about to leave when we were called back and asked to take seats in the adjoining room, where we could hear everything that was said. I remember the Englishman asked General Lee whom he thought the greatest military genius developed by the war, to which General Lee answered without hesitation "General N. B. Forrest, of Tennessee, whom I have never met. He accomplished more with fewer troops than any other officer on either side."

When Lord Wolseley took his departure we were called in. Graham at once said: "I heard, General, what you said this morning before chapel." He then told about his missing wood and the course he had pursued to find out who was stealing it, winding up his remarks, "But, General, I didn't know that it was Prof. Joynes."

This was one of the very few times I've seen the General laugh. To close the incident he said, "Well, Mr. Graham, your plan to find out who was taking your wood was a good one, but your powder charge was too heavy. The next time use less powder."

RILEY, *After Appomattox, pp. 70-72.*

The Feeling of Awe Left Me at the Threshold of His Door

John B. Collyar of Nashville, Tennessee, presents a college boy's observation of General Lee.

A few years after General Lee accepted the presidency of the then Washington College, I was sent to be entered in the preparatory department, along with an older brother who was to enter college. The morning after we reached Lexington we repaired to the office of General Lee, situated in the college building, for the purpose of matriculation and receiving instructions as to the duties devolving upon us as students. I entered the office with

The President of Washington College. *From a photograph by Boude and Miley, Lexington, Virginia, late 1869. Reproduced from the collection of the Dementi Studio, Richmond, Va.*

reverential awe, expecting to see the great warrior, whose fame then encircled the civilized globe, as I had pictured him in my own imagination. General Lee was alone, looking over a paper. He arose as we entered, and received us with a quiet, gentlemanly dignity that was so natural and easy and kind that the feeling of awe left me at the threshold of his door.

General Lee had but one manner in his intercourse with men. It was the same to the peasant as to the prince, and the student was received with the easy courtliness that would have been bestowed on the greatest imperial dignitary of Europe.

I do not know that I could define the impression that General Lee left on my mind that morning. . . . He was so gentle, kind, and almost motherly, in his bearing, that I thought there must be some mistake about it. At first glance General Lee's countenance was stern, but the moment his eye met that of his entering guest it beamed with a kindness that at once established easy and friendly relations, but not familiar. The impression he made on me was, that he was never familiar with any man.

I saw General Lee every day during the session in chapel (for he never missed a morning service) and passing through the campus to and from his home to his office. He rarely spoke to any one—occasionally would say something to one of the boys as he passed, but never more than a word. After the first morning in his office he never spoke to me but once. He stopped me one morning as I was passing his front gate and asked how I was getting on with my studies. I replied to his inquiry, and that was the end of the conversation. He seemed to avoid contact with men, and the impression which he made on me, seeing him every day, and which has since clung to me, strengthening the impression then made, was, that he was bowed down with a broken heart. I never saw a sadder expression than General Lee carried during the entire time I was there. It looked as if the sorrow of a whole nation had been collected in his countenance, and as if he was bearing the grief of his whole people. It never left his face, but was ever there to keep company with the kindly smile. . . . The old iron-gray horse was the privileged character at General Lee's home. He was permitted to remain in the front yard where the grass was greenest and freshest, notwithstanding the flowers and shrubbery. General Lee was more demonstrative toward that old companion in battle than seemed to be in his intercourse with men. I have often seen him, as he would enter his front gate, leave the walk, approach the old horse, and caress him for a minute or two before entering his front door, as though they bore a common grief in their memory of the past.

RILEY, *After Appomattox, pp. 65-68.*

Traveller

Young Collyar was quite correct in his observation. Lee was passionately fond of his wartime companion. For his cousin, Martha Custis Williams, who was painting Traveller's portrait, he wrote the following sensitive description.

If I was an artist like you, I would draw a true picture of Traveller; representing his fine proportions, muscular figure, deep chest, short back, strong haunches, flat legs, small head, broad forehead, delicate ears, quick eye, small feet, & black mane & tail. Such a picture would inspire a poet, whose genius could then depict his worth, & describe his endurance of toil, hunger, thirst, heat & cold; & the dangers & suffering through which he has passed. He could dilate upon his sagacity & affection, & his invariable response to every wish of his rider. He might even imagine his thoughts through the long night-Marches & days of battle through which he has passed. But I am no artist Markie, & can therefore only say he is a Confederate *grey*. To your other questions I can give more definite answers. I purchased him in the mountains of Virginia in the Fall of 1861, & he has been my patient follower ever since, to Georgia, the Carolinas & back to Virginia. He carried me through the seven days battle around Richmond, the Second Manassas, at Sharpsburg, Fredericksburg, the last day at Chancellorsville, to Penna, at Gettysburg, & back to the Rappahannock. From the commencement of the campaign in 1864 at Orange, till its close around

Petersburg, the saddle was scarcely off his back, as he passed through the fire of the Wilderness, Spotsylvania, Cold Harbour & across the James River. He was almost in daily requisition in the winter of 1864 '65 on the long line of defences from the Chickahominy north of Richmond, to Hatchers run south of the Appomattox, 35 miles in length; & in 1865 bore me to the final day at Appomattox Ct House. You know the comfort he is to me in my present retirement. He is well supplied with equipments—Two sets have been sent to him from England, one by the Ladies in Baltimore & one was made for him in Richmond; but I think his favorite, is the American saddle from St. Louis. Of all his companions in toil, *Richmond, Brown-Roan, Ajax* & quiet *Lucy Long*, he is the only one that retained his vigour to the last. The two first expired under their onerous burden, & the two last failed—You can I am sure from what I have said paint his portrait—

"To Markie," pp. 73-75.

Three Cheers and a Tiger for the Heroes

Young John Collyar reported that during the entire time he was at Washington College General Lee carried so sad an expression on his face that it looked as if he bore the grief of all his people and was bowed down with a broken heart. Again the student was undoubtedly right. Notwithstanding his remarkable physique, the general's heart was damaged by the strain of war, and, in the five years following Appomattox, he aged rapidly and prematurely.

In March, 1870, yielding to the solicitation of friends and medical advisers, he made a six weeks' visit to Georgia and Florida. The trip was expected to improve his health, but far from attaining this goal, it turned into an exhausting hero's progress through the Southern states which, no doubt, hastened the end. But however difficult it must have been for him to endure the pain and suffering entailed by this journey, the adoration, love and respect accorded him by the people brought a full measure of happiness to the afternoon of his life.

From Richmond, Lee accompanied by his daughter, Agnes, went first to Warrenton, North Carolina, to visit the grave of his youngest daughter, Annie, who had died in 1862 and was buried at Warrenton Springs. After a night and a day, the Lees were again headed southward. Word had gone before them and at station after station people were waiting. Agnes described this remarkable journey in a letter to her mother.

We spent that night in the sleeping car, very handsome and comfortable, but the novelty, I suppose, made us wakeful. At Raleigh and another place people crowded to the depot and called "Lee! Lee!" and cheered vociferously, but we were locked up and "mum." Everywhere along the road where meals were provided the landlords invited us in, and when we would not get out, sent coffee and lunches. Even soldiers on the train sent in fruit, and I think we were expected to die of eating. At Charlotte and Salisbury there were crowds and bands. Colonel [J. L.] Corley joined us at [Charlotte], having asked to go to Savannah with us. The train stopped fifteen minutes at Columbia. Colonel Alexander Haskell took charge of the crowd, which, in spite of the pouring rain, stood there till we left. General E. Porter Alexander was there, and was very hearty in his inquiries after all of us. His little girl was lifted into the car. Namesakes appeared on the way, of all sizes. Old ladies stretched their heads into the windows at way-stations, and then drew back and said "He is mightily like his pictures." We reached Augusta Wednesday night. The mayor and council met us, having heard a few minutes before that papa was on the train. We were whirled off to the hotel, and papa decided to spend Thursday there. They had a reception the whole of the morning. Crowds came. Wounded soldiers, servants, and working-men even. The sweetest little children—namesakes—dressed to their eyes, with bouquets of japonica—or tiny cards in their little fat hands—with their names. . . . At some point on the way here [to Savannah] Generals [A. R.] Lawton and [J. F.] Gilmer, Mr. Andrew Lowe, and others, got on the cars with us. Flowers were given us at various places. I so much enjoyed the evidences of spring all along our route—more and more advanced as we proceeded. The jasmine, though passing away, was still in sufficient abundance, in some places, to perfume the air. The dark marshes were rich in tall magnolia trees, beautiful red buds, and other red blossoms I did not know. The jasmine and the trees hanging with gray moss—perfectly weird-looking— have been the least luxuriant places in the interim. Savannah is green with live-oaks—and filled with trees and shrubbery. I wish you could see a large marble table in the parlour, where I am writing, with a pyramid of jasmine in the centre and four large plates full at the corners, almost covering the square, all sent me Saturday. The Lawtons are as kind as possible, wanted papa to stay here, but Mr. Andrew Lowe had arranged to take him to his house at bedtime. So he lost the benefit of a serenade from two bands, alternating, which we enjoyed—General Lawton telling the crowd General Lee had retired from fatigue. . . .

AGNES LEE TO MARY LEE, Savannah, Ga., April 3, 1870
in R. E. Lee, Jr., *Recollection and Letters, pp. 391-394.*

Savannah was probably the high point in Lee's remarkable journey, and as he left the train he had to face one of the largest crowds ever assembled to welcome him. In addition to the townspeople, the throng included hundreds of Confederate veterans, former Negro slaves, and the Federal army of occupation. Cheer followed cheer until the General had to rise and bow his acknowledgments.

Demonstrations of affection continued long into the night. Said the Savannah Morning News:

Gentlemen, representing socially and materially the young men of Savannah, and desiring to pay their old leader a social visit, engaged the Saxe Horn and Washington Cornet bands, and at ten o'clock assembled at the Metropolitan Fire Company engine house. . . .

The procession made its way noiselessly to the residence of General Lawton, and by the time it had reached the house it had swollen to an enthusiastic crowd of young men, all of whom were exceedingly anxious to get a glimpse of the old hero, under whom all of them had served.

Arriving at the house the band played "Hail to the Chief" and "Dixie" with other tunes, but the General, having retired, being very unwell, Gen. Lawton appeared, and in his behalf thanked the gentlemen for the compliment, stating that Gen. Lee would have an opportunity of taking them by the hand during the course of his stay in Savannah. With three rousing cheers and a tiger for the hero, the procession . . . which now numbered fully one thousand, proceeded to the residence of Gen. Joseph E. Johnston, next to Gen. Lee the greatest soldier of modern times.

The General, hearing the sound of martial music; beat a retreat in masterly style.

The party serenaded General Johnston, playing "Dixie," "Bonnie Blue Flag," and other national airs, and wound up with three rousing cheers and a tiger for General Joseph E. Johnston.

From thence the procession proceeded to the residence of General Henry R. Jackson, and after playing several airs, the General made his appearance, and in a very stirring speech paid high tribute to the two greatest of living generals and patriots.

With the same compliment to General Jackson, the procession then marched to the residence of Colonel John Screven, Mayor, and played several tunes. Col. Screven, being sick, did not make his appearance, and after several airs had been played, of course, including "Dixie," Captain Dillon proposed three cheers for Col. John Screven, and they were given with a hearty good will.

We have never known a program so successfully carried out.

Savannah Morning News, April 2, 1870.

On a Quiet Autumn Morning

October 12, 1870, General Lee died at Lexington, Virginia.

On a quiet autumn morning in the land he loved so well, and, as he held, served so faithfully, the spirit of Robert Edward Lee, left the clay which it had so much enobled, and travelled out of this world into the great and mysterious land. Yesterday the expressions of regret which sprang from the few who surrounded the bedside of the dying soldier and Christian will be swelled today into one mighty voice of sorrow, resounding throughout our country and extending over all parts of the world where his great genius and many virtues are known. For not to the Southern people alone shall be limited the tribute of a tear over the dead Virginian. Here in the North, forgetting that the time was when the sword of Robert Edward Lee was drawn against us—forgetting and forgiving all the years of bloodshed and agony—, we have long since ceased to look upon him as the Confederate leader, but have claimed him as one of ourselves; have cherished and felt proud of his military genius as belonging to us; have recounted his triumphs as our own; have extolled his virtues as reflecting honor upon us — for Robert Edward Lee was an American. . . .

Never had a mother a nobler son. In him the military genius of America was developed to a greater extent than ever before. In him all that was pure and lofty in mind and purpose found lodgment. Dignified without presumption, affable, without familiarity, he united all of the charms of manners which made him the idol of his friends and of his soldiers, and won for him the respect and admiration of the world. Even as in the days of his triumph, glory did not intoxicate, so when the dark clouds swept over him, adversity did not depress. From the hour that he surrendered his sword at Appomattox to the fatal autumn morning, he passed among men noble in his quiet, simple dignity, displaying neither bitterness nor regret over the irrevocable past. He conquered us in misfortune by the grand manner in which he sustained himself, even as he dazzled us by his genius when the tramp of his soldiers resounded through the valleys of Virginia.

And for such a man we are all tears and sorrow today. Standing beside his grave men of the South and men of the North can mourn with all the bitterness of four years of warfare erased by this common bereavement.

New York Herald, October 13, 1870.

As news of the death of Lee spread through the South each community was plunged into profound sorrow. Business houses were closed with crepe upon the doors. In Lexington, Virginia, even the colored barbers shut up their shops. Schools and colleges suspended activities, and church bells rang out mournful dirges. An expression of deep grief was visible in every face. Yet the end of the great Chieftain was not unexpected.

General Lee had been almost entirely unconscious since Monday night last, and expired very peacefully and quietly at half past nine o'clock, Wednesday morning. He was first taken sick on Wednesday evening, September 28th, while just about to sit down to tea, when he suddenly sank in his chair insensible. He soon reacted, and in the course of the next ten days steadily improved, until it was hoped he was out of danger. But on Monday evening last he became suddenly and rapidly worse, and continued to sink until Wednesday morning.

During the early part of his sickness he slept much and spoke but little, but was rational when awake, and always recognized those who approached him. At times his mind seemed for a little while to wander, and, on several occasions he reverted to the army. He once ordered his tent to be struck and at another time desired that Hill should be sent for. He suffered comparatively little pain during his whole sickness and died without a struggle. He will be buried on Saturday, October 15th, at 12 o'clock. The place selected for the interment is a vault beneath the College Chapel which stands in the midst of the College grounds.

Savannah Morning News, October 14, 1870. Dateline: "Lexington, Va., October 13."

The passing of Lee was noted throughout the world. Of the many foreign tributes, one of the most graceful came from England.

Few are the generals who have earned, since history began, a greater military reputation. Still fewer are the men of similar eminence, civil or military, whose personal qualities would bear comparison with his. The bitterest enemies of his country hardly dared to whisper a word against the character of her most distinguished general, while neutrals regarded him with an admiration for his deeds and a respect for his lofty and unselfish nature which almost grew into veneration, and his own countrymen learned to look up to him with as much confidence and esteem as they ever felt for Washington, and with an affection which the cold demeanor and austere temper of Washington could never inspire. . . . Truer greatness, a loftier nature, a spirit more unselfish, a character purer, more chivalrous the world has rarely if ever known. Of stainless life and deep religious feeling, yet free from all taint of cant and fanaticism, and as dear and congenial to the Cavalier Stuart as to the Puritan Stonewall Jackson. Unambitious, but ready to sacrifice all at the call of duty; devoted to his cause, yet never moved by his feelings beyond the line prescribed by his judgment; never provoked by just resentment to punish wanton cruelty by reprisals, which would have given a character of needless savagery to the war—both North and South owe a deep debt of gratitude to him, and the time will come when both will be equally proud of him. And well they may, for his character and life afford a complete answer to the reproaches commonly cast on money grubbing, mechanical America. A country which has given birth to men like him, and those who followed him, may look the chivalry of Europe in the face without shame, for the fatherlands of Sidney and Bayard never produced a nobler soldier, gentleman, and Christian than Robert E. Lee.

London Standard. Quoted in Savannah Morning News, October 25, 1870.

Our Life is But as a Shadow, a Dream

I should have written sooner My dear Miss Mackay to acknowledge the kind & most welcome letters from Mrs. Elliott & yourself as well as the one enclosed but if you knew how many I have had to write with rather feeble hands you would excuse me for since I have read in the life of Mr. George Prentiss that he lost the use of his hand from constant writing I have feared to add that to the rest of my infirmities as the use of my pen affords me great pleasure in holding converse with friends whom perhaps I shall never more see for in this isolated spot very few can come to me & I cannot go to them. I rejoiced as much as you did that Gen. Lee was able to visit his old friends in Savannah where he had met with so much kindness in his younger days & spoke to me so often of every member of your family that I felt as if I knew them all. Your sister Margaret seemed to have been an especial favorite & perhaps it was well for me that her affections were then engaged. I was reading a few days ago all his old letters to me from Savannah & it seemed but as yesterday the time when I was always so anxiously expecting them. I can now indeed realize so forcibly the scripture that our life is but as a shadow, a dream. God is merciful in gradually loosening our ties to earth.

M. C. Lee to Miss Catherine Mackay, *Lexington, Va., February 2, 1871.* MS in possession of Miss Clermont Lee, Savannah, Georgia.

Epilogue
A Small and Crowded Planet

Address of General Edward Porter Alexander, on Alumni Day, West Point Centennial, June 9, 1902.

And now a generation has passed away. The smoke of civil conflict has vanished forever from the sky, and the whole country, under the new conditions evolved in its four years' struggle, finds itself united in developing its vast resources in successful rivalry with the greatest nations of the earth. . . . The right to secede, the stake for which we fought so desperately, were it now offered as a gift, we would reject as we would a proposition of suicide. . . .

We believed, and still believe, that its sovereignty was intended to be reserved by each and every State when it ratified the Constitution. It was universally taught among us that in this feature there was divinely inspired wisdom. It may have been wisdom for that century. Each State was then an independent agricultural community. The railroad, the steamship, the telegraph, were undreamed of on earth. But, as in nature, whenever the climate has changed, the fauna and flora have been forced to change and adapt themselves to the new environment, so among mankind must modes of government be modified to conform to new conditions. . . .

. . . This is but a small and crowded planet, now that science has brought its ends together by her great inventions. Neither states nor nations can longer dwell to themselves. An irrepressible conflict is on between barbarism and civilization. Through human imperfection much that must be done may seem harsh and cruel. Much that has happened doubtless was so to our aborigines; but for all that we must look forward and not backward, and walk bodly in the paths of progress.

.   .   .   .

But there is still one thing more to be said. Was all our blood shed in vain? Was all the agony endured for the Lost Cause but as water spilled upon the sand? No! A thousand times, no!

We have set the world record for devotion to a cause. We have given our children proud memories, and to history new names, to be a theme and an inspiration for unborn generations. The heroes of future wars will emulate our "Lees and Jacksons." We have taught the armies of the world the casualties to be endured in battle. But above and beyond all, the firm bonds which today hold together this great nation could have never been wrought by debates in Congress. Human evolution has not yet progressed so far. Such bonds must be forged, welded, and proved in the heat of battle and must be cemented in blood.

. . . We didn't *go* into our cause; we were *born* into it. We fought it out to its remotest end and suffered to the very utmost its dying aches and pains. But they were rich in compensations and have proven to be only the birth-pangs of a new nation, in whose career we are proud to own and to bear a part.

Address of General E. P. Alexander, On Alumni Day, West Point Centennial, June 9, 1902.

Bibliography

Manuscripts

Frank B. Screven typescript, "The Letters of R. E. Lee to the Mackay Family," Georgia Historical Society, Savannah.

R. E. Lee Letters and Papers relating to his military career, National Archives.

Letters from R. E. Lee and his wife to Mrs. William Henry Stiles, Robert E. Lee Memorial Foundation, Inc., Stratford Hall Plantation, Virginia.

Letter from R. E. Lee to Capt. Andrew J. Talcott, Virginia Historical Society Richmond.

R. E. Lee Letters, drawing, and plans, Fort Pulaski National Monument.

Publications

Acton, John, First Baron, *Selections from the correspondence of John Emerich Edward Dalberg Acton,* The Macmillan Company, New York, 1922.

Alexander, E. P., *Military Memoirs of a Confederate.* Charles Scribner's Sons, New York, 1907.

........................., "Personal Recollections of the Break-up of the Confederacy," *Century Illustrated Monthly Magazine,* Vol. 63, No. 6, April, 1902.

........................., *Address on Alumni Day, West Point Centennial, June 9, 1902.* Pamphlet "Presented with the compliments of the Burrows Brothers Company, Ohio." Republican Printing Company, Cedar Rapids, Iowa n.d.

Andrews, Marietta M. *Scraps of Paper.* E. P. Dutton & Co., New York, 1929.

Cooke, John Esten, *A Life of General Robert E. Lee.* D. Appleton & Company, New York, 1871.

Craven, Avery, ed., *"To Markie," The Letters of Robert E. Lee to Martha Custis Williams.* Harvard University Press, Cambridge, 1933.

Freeman, Douglas Southall, *R. E. Lee: A Biography,* 4 vols. Charles Scribner's Sons, New York, 1934-35.

........................, ed., *Lee's Dispatches, Unpublished Letters of General Robert E. Lee, C. S. A., to Jefferson Davis and the War Department of the Confederate States of America, 1862-65.* G. P. Putnam's Sons, New York, 1915.

........................, "Lee and the Ladies," *Scribner's Magazine,* October, 1925.

Fremantle, Lt. Col. A. J. L.; *Three Months in the Southern States, April-June, 1863.* William Blackwood and Sons, Edinburgh and London, 1863.

Gordon, John B., *Reminiscences of the Civil War.* Charles Scribner's Sons, New York, 1903.

Grant, Ulysses S., *Personal Memoirs,* 2 vols. Charles Webster & Company New York, 1885-86.

Jones, J. B., *A Rebel War Clerk's Diary,* 2 vols. J. B. Lippincott Company, Philadelphia, 1866.

Jones, J. William, *Personal Reminiscences, Anecdotes, and Letters of General Robert E. Lee.* D. Appleton & Company, New York, 1875.

............................, *Life and Letters of Robert Edward Lee, Soldier and Man.* The Neale Publishing Company, New York and Washington, 1906.

Lee, Edmund Jennings, *Lee of Virgina,* Vol. II. Philadelphia, 1895.

Lee, Fitzhugh, *General Lee.* D. Appleton & Company, New York, 1894.

Lee, Captain Robert E., [Jr.], *Recollections and Letters of General Robert E. Lee.* Doubleday, Page & Company, New York, 1904.

Lee, Robert E., ed., Third Edition of Henry Lee's *Memoirs of the War in the Southern Department of the United States,* University Publishing Company, New York, 1870.

Long, A. L., *Memoirs of Robert E. Lee.* J. M. Stoddart & Company, New York, 1886.

Longstreet, James, *From Manassas to Appomattox, Memoirs of the Civil War in America.* J. B. Lippincott Company, Philadelphia, 1896.

Marshall, Charles, "Appomattox." An address delivered before the Society of the Army and Navy of the Confederate States in the State of Maryland on Jan. 19, 1894. Privately printed and circulated. Reprinted in *Century Illustrated Monthly Magazine,* Vol. 63, No. 6 (April, 1902).

Mason, Emily V., *Popular Life of Robert Edward Lee.* 2nd rev. ed. John Murphy and Co., Baltimore, 1872.

Maury, Dabney H., *Recollection of a Virginian in the Mexican, Indian and Civil Wars.* Charles Scribner's Sons, New York, 1894.

Myers, Frank M., *The Comanches. A History of White's Battalion, Virginia Cavalry.* Kelly, Piet & Co., Baltimore, 1871.

Riley, Franklin L., *General Robert E. Lee After Appomattox.* The Macmillan Company, New York, 1922.

Taylor, Walter H., *Four Years With General Lee.* D. Appleton and Co., New York, 1877.

............................, *General Lee, His Campaigns in Virginia, 1861-1865.* Nusbaum Book and News Company, Norfolk, 1906.

War of the Rebellion: a Compilation of the Official Records of the Union and Confederate Armies. 130 vols. Washington, Government Printing Office, 1880-1901.

[Wolseley, Garnett, later Viscount Wolseley], "A Month's Visit to the Confederate Headquarters," *Blackwood's Edinburgh Magazine,* Vol. 93, No. 567 (January, 1863).

Newspapers

Savannah Morning News, June, 1862; April and October, 1870.
New York Herald, October, 1870.

Acknowledgments . . .

The Publications Committee, Eastern National Park and Monument Association (Chairman, Rogers W. Young; Members, Benjamin H. Davis and Ralston B. Lattimore), which directed the production of this publication, and the author, wish to acknowledge, on behalf of the Association, the gracious assistance and permission given by the following individuals, organizations, and publishers:

Individuals

Mrs. Hunter de Butts, Upperville, Virginia, and Mrs. Hanson Ely, Richmond, Virginia, granddaughters of Robert E. Lee, provided the daguerreotypes and photographs of the Lee children and gave permission to reproduce them in this book.

Mrs. Screven Duke, New York, gave us, in memory of her mother, Mrs. Frank B. Screven, the original letter from Lee to Eliza A. Mackay, dated April 13, 1831, and made available to us many transcripts of other letters of Lee to the Mackay family. Mrs. Screven Duke is a great granddaughter of Eliza Mackay Stiles.

Mrs. Douglas Southall Freeman, Richmond, Virginia, graciously permitted us to examine and quote the original letter of Robert E. Lee to Capt. Andrew J. Talcott, July 13, 1831.

Mrs. Thomas Hilton, Savannah, Georgia, made available to us articles, books, and addresses by her grandfather, General E. P. Alexander.

Miss Clermont Lee, Savannah, Georgia, allowed us to quote from the letter of Margaret Cowper Mackay Elliott to Lucy Trowbridge, dated April 1870, and the letter from M. C. Lee to Catherine Mackay, dated February 2, 1871. Miss Lee is a great granddaughter of Margaret Mackay Elliott.

Mr. Charles F. Mills, Atherton, California, allowed us to reproduce the original drawing of "Napoleon" made by Lee and presented to Margaret Mackay on her wedding day, June 29, 1830. Mr. Mills is a great grandson of Eliza Mackay Stiles.

Mr. Carter Lee Refo, Richmond, Virginia, permitted us to photograph in color and reproduce his original Gilbert Stuart painting of Maj. Gen. Henry ("Light Horse Harry") Lee, the father of Robert E. Lee.

Mr. Frank B. Screven, Clearwater, Florida, permitted us to quote from his typescript entitled "The Letters of R. E. Lee to the Mackay Family," in the Georgia Historical Society, Savannah.

The author acknowledges with thanks the valuable assistance rendered to him by Mrs. Forman M. Hawes, Director of the Georgia Historical Society, and by the Reference Staff of the Savannah Public Library. He is especially indebted to Walter C. Hartridge, past president of the Georgia Historical Society, for his critical reading of the manuscript and proof sheets, and to his many colleagues in the Southeast Regional Office and the Washington Office of the National Park Service, without whose help this book would not have been possible.

Organizations

The engraving, Lee on Traveller in Battle, 1863, is used through the courtesy of the Confederate Museum, Richmond, Virginia.

The Georgia Historical Society, Savannah, Georgia, made available to us its fine collection of manuscripts, typescripts, and newspapers.

Robert E. Lee Memorial Foundation, Inc., permitted us to use the original Robert E. Lee letters in the library of Stratford Hall, Westmoreland County, Virginia, the birthplace of Robert E. Lee.

Miss Virginia Daiker, Library of Congress, and Miss Josephine Cobb, National Archives, rendered valuable assistance to us in securing drawings and photographs from these institutions.

National Park Service—Mr. James W. Holland, Regional Historian; Mr. Roger J. Rogers, Regional Publications Officer; Mr. Hubert A. Gurney (deceased); and Miss Ruth Pridham; all on the staff of the Southeast Regional Office at Richmond, Virginia; are thanked for their fine editorial endeavors which contributed so materially to the content of this publication. Mrs. Agnes Mullins, Custis-Lee Mansion, Arlington, Virginia, also was very helpful in securing copies of the Lee Coat-of-Arms and Lee photographs and assisted with helpful advice. National Capital Region, National Park Service, Washington, D. C., gave permission to reproduce the Benson J. Lossing water color entitled "Arlington House," in the museum of the Custis-Lee Mansion, Arlington, Virginia. Miss Lillian Cash, Washington Office helped with many details.

The Smithsonian Institution, Washington, D. C., permitted us to reproduce the George Catlin paintings, Steamboat "Yellow Stone" leaving St. Louis, and "The Prairies Enveloped in Flames and Smoke." The plate for the latter painting used in *George Catlin and the Old Frontier*, by Harold McCracken, was loaned to the Association by The Dial Press. New York.

Virginia Historical Society, Richmond, Virginia, allowed us to quote from the letter of Robert E. Lee to Capt. Andrew J. Talcott, May 5, 1836; and to reproduce the portrait of Gen. Robert E. Lee, as he appears in the Hoffbauer mural at Battle Abbey, Richmond, Virginia, on the cover of this publication.

Washington and Lee University, Lexington, Virginia, granted us permission to make color photographs and to reproduce the William E. West portraits of Lt. and Mrs. Robert E. Lee, in the Lee Memorial Chapel.

Publishers

The Association greatly appreciates the kind permission to quote from the following published works:

Selections from the Correspondence of John Emerich Edward Dalberg Acton, by John Acton, First Baron, The Macmillan Company, New York, 1922.

General Robert E. Lee After Appomattox, by Franklin L. Riley, The Macmillan Company, New York, 1922 (published as a memorial by Washington and Lee University). Additional permission granted by Edward M. Riley, Williamsburg, Virginia.

Lee's Dispatches: Unpublished Letters of General Robert E. Lee, C.S.A. to Jefferson Davis and the War Department of the Confederate States of America 1862-1865, by Douglas Southall Freeman, Copyright 1915, G. P. Putnam's Sons, New York.

Scraps of Paper, by Marietta M. Andrews, Copyright 1929 by E. P. Dutton and Co., Inc., New York; renewal, 1957, by American Security & Trust Company.

The excerpts from MILITARY MEMOIRS OF A CONFEDERATE, by E. P. Alexander (Copyright 1907, Charles Scribner's Sons, New York; renewal copyright 1935) and R. E. LEE: A BIOGRAPHY, by Douglas S. Freeman (Copyright 1935, Charles Scribner's Sons) are reprinted with the permission of Charles Scribner's Sons.

To Markie: The Letters of Robert E. Lee to Martha Custis Williams, Avery Craven, Editor, Harvard University Press, Cambridge, 1933, pp. 56-60 and 73-74; permission granted by the Henry E. Huntington Library and Art Gallery, San Marino, California.